ghosted

DATING & OTHER PARAMOURAL EXPERIENCES

ghosted

DATING & OTHER PARAMOURAL EXPERIENCES

JANA EISENSTEIN

atmosphere press

Dedication

My grandfather was the first great storyteller I ever knew. Every summer as a small child, I would visit him and my grandma at their bungalow in the Catskills and look forward to the tales he would spin at my bedside to lull me to sleep. Sometimes he related fables, like "The Ant and the Cricket" or "The Tortoise and the Hare"; other times he created fairy tales starring a princess named Jana. Those were my favorite.

During the day, when we weren't out picking berries in the woods nearby, swimming in the bungalow colony's pool with the other grandparents and grandchildren, or snagging a bargain at the local flea market, he would sit with me and encourage me to write my own stories. It wasn't until after he died and we were sorting through his things that I discovered my grandfather had saved them all. He's the reason I started writing at an early age, and why I enjoy it to this day.

Table of Contents

PART 3: Haunted

/ˈgōst/

verb

1. abruptly cut off all contact with someone (such as a former romantic partner) by no longer accepting or responding to phone calls, instant messages, etc.[1]

2. let someone know you think so little of them that you can't even bother to reject them from afar

past tense: **ghosted***; past participle:* **ghosted**

1. hang out in the bathtub with a bottle of vodka till enough time has elapsed that it's clear the person is no longer speaking to you

---

[1] "Ghost." *Merriam-Webster.com Dictionary*, Merriam-Webster, https://www.merriam-webster.com/dictionary/ghost. Accessed 18 Apr. 2021.

Part 1

BUMP IN THE NIGHT

EQUAL OPPORTUNITY EXPLOITER

How did I get here? I wondered one particularly hazy morning as I sketched a crude map showing the path from my apartment to the Metro station, marking all the important landmarks: the port-a-potty up the block, the group of homeless people at the corner, and the abandoned row houses lining the next street. I finished my map, tore it out of my notebook, and handed it to the guy in my bed.

"Follow the arrows to the Mount Vernon station." I spoke slowly and loudly, emphasizing each word. "You can switch to the red line at Chinatown." To make my point, I tapped the sheet of paper where I had written the word *Chinatown.*

He looked at me sleepily but made no movement to indicate he understood.

"Ok then." I started walking out of my bedroom, hoping he'd follow. "Time to go." In a last-ditch effort to get my point across, I began pointing to him, to the stairs, then back to him. He stood and dressed slowly, clearly in no rush to leave. Stepping into the living room, he paused again to look around. Though we had spent a few minutes there the night before, he hadn't been in a state of mind to take in the hardwood floors, high ceiling, or beautiful skylights.

As he looked up at the morning sun streaking through those skylights, I took the opportunity to place my hand on his back and guide him to the stairs. He descended the first two steps and looked back at me. I didn't want to give him the impression that I'd be walking him to the Metro, so I just stood there waving from the top step. I could see the message finally sink in, and a few seconds later I heard the welcome sound of the door shutting behind him. I dragged myself over to the couch and plopped down. *How did I get here?* I wondered again.

I woke up on the couch a half hour later to the sounds of my roommate and best friend, Kat, making breakfast. She brought a bowl of dry cereal and a cup of coffee over to the couch and sat down without saying a word. She turned to me, mug in hand, and smiled.

"Soooo? How was last night?" she finally inquired with a mischievous grin.

I looked at her accusingly. "So, you knew?" Even to myself I sounded tired.

She laughed. "Yeah. Didn't you?"

"Not till I got him home."

"How did you miss that? You were dancing with him for like an hour." I didn't care for the glee in her voice.

"Yeah, he was a pretty great dancer..." I began to remember, almost fondly. Then it all started to make sense.

We spent the previous night at Irish Times, a chill bar near Union Station in DC with a dance club in the basement. I vaguely remembered a large group of exuberant people my age gesturing to one another as they danced. They all had better rhythm than I did, which truthfully, didn't take much. I was enjoying the night with some grad school friends, jumping up and down and screaming along to Kelly Clarkson's "Since U Been Gone," channeling the rage I had yet to actually experience, when a cute guy with red hair and a matching ginger beard appeared and wrapped his arms around my waist.

Feeling empowered by Ms. Clarkson's bold words, I smiled at the guy and complimented his moves. He smiled back, and we chatted for a bit as we danced. Well, chatted was perhaps a bit inaccurate. The music was exceptionally loud in the cement-walled basement bar, so we just mouthed words back and forth to each other, grinding our hips together under the guise of dancing.

After what I'm sure was an uncomfortably long time for the people around us, my date-for-the-night removed his hands from my ass and led me to the bar at the back of the dimly lit dance floor. In a move that should have struck me as unusual, he pulled out his license and pointed to his name. I racked my brain now to remember what it was, but in the light of day I knew it really didn't matter.

After flashing his ID, he smiled, pointed at me, and asked, "You?" Without batting an eye, I pulled out my license and showed him my name. Or maybe he was checking my age? I was certainly acting like a drunken teenager.

He winked at me, then wove his way through the crowd to the bar, returning a few minutes later with two drinks. I accepted a beer and back to the dance floor we went. Though smoking had been banned in all bars and clubs in DC for years, the basement air still stunk of stale cigarettes and hung humid and heavy around us. The thick haze, combined with the booze and familiar hooks of the bubbly music set the mood for our very public, very aggressive make-out session.

The details got fuzzier from there. But, as the lights came on for last call around 1:40 a.m., a few of his friends came by, I assume to let us know they were leaving and to inquire about his plans for the night. Realizing how late it was, I scanned the bar for my own friends.

Spotting my group at the bar, paying their tabs, I tried to get their attention to indicate I, too, was ready to go. Once they acknowledged my limp-wristed waving, I returned my attention to my date to say a proper goodbye. With my tongue. But when I turned back around, his friends were already gone. My date took my hand, looked deep into my glassy eyes, and confidently mouthed the words, "I'm coming home with you." I nodded and resumed my position on his face.

My classmates, my date, and I were kicked out of the bar at 2 a.m., and we all stumbled to the nearest Metro station together. At that hour, the trains were running every twenty minutes, and we had just missed ours. As we waited for the next train, my friends gave the two of us a wide berth, more for their sake than mine. At the time, I thought my new acquaintance and I were getting along splendidly, sharing tales about each other's childhoods, revealing our deepest thoughts and dreams. Upon re-evaluation, I'm not sure we ever attempted to speak to one another. When we weren't making out, we leaned on each other in silence until the train arrived.

Kat, my date, and I split from the rest of our group at Chinatown and took the Yellow Line to the Mt. Vernon station. I held his hand as Kat and I briskly led the way to our apartment. My neighborhood wasn't the place to take a stroll after dark. We paused to wave to Lil' Ricky, the de facto leader of the homeless troupe that lived on our street corner. He stepped out from behind the bushes and waved back, eyeing my unfamiliar suitor.

Lil' Ricky, a middle-aged man with white patches in his beard and unwashed curly hair, was very protective of me, referring to me often as his wife. Though fairly certain it wasn't legally binding, I didn't dare contest the claim. Because of his fondness for me, he didn't approve of the occasional men I brought home and offered to "take care" of anyone who treated me poorly. At the time, I was touched. Guys I had relationships with rarely offered to pay, let alone kill for me.

But, at that hour, with that memory in mind, I ushered Kat and my new friend away from Lil' Ricky's gaze. We hurried past the port-a-potty—often used for warmth or sex by Lil' Ricky's companions after dark—keys in hand. Once we were safe inside our apartment, Kat retreated to her bedroom, leaving me and my date alone in the living room. For some reason, he felt comfortable enough to hop onto my laptop, which I had left open on the coffee table, and start poking around. I should have been angered by this invasion of privacy or annoyed by how quickly he made himself at home, but at that time of night and after that many drinks, I wasn't feeling much of anything.

Unfazed, I decided I should get to know this stranger I had brought home with me. Sitting beside him on the arm of the sofa, I began with a simple question: "So, what do you do? Are you in school?"

No response.

I repeated my question. Nothing.

I tried a different tack. "Where do you live?" Crickets. He was staring at my Facebook page. Ok, now he was just being rude. Or maybe he was ignoring me as some weird power move?

Annoyed, I tapped his shoulder. As he turned, I shrugged and put my hands out in front of me in the universal gesture for "what's going on?" He looked at me as if I was an idiot, pointed to his ear, and said, "I'm deaf."

Hoooly shit. My drunken mind was racing. Well, not racing. Wobbling. I was like a two-year-old trying to piece this puzzle together—determined, but incapable. *Had there been clues?*

But before my weary mind could focus on the many, obvious signs—like the fact that he had asked me my name by inquiring to see my license, or that the emphatic gesturing I had noticed at the beginning of the night had actually been people signing to one another—it was distracted with another thought. *Is it rude to ask him to leave?* I wondered, not because he was deaf, but because this realization made me acutely aware of the fact that I knew nothing about this man sitting next to me. He was no longer the hot guy I had spent all night dancing with. He was a stranger.

With no coherent exit strategy in place, and emboldened by some excessive intoxication and moderate curiosity, I dismissed my concerns. My immediate solution was to pull out some paper and a pen so I could let him know in no uncertain terms that I needed him out of my apartment first thing in the morning. It would have been too cruel to leave him out on the street with Lil' Ricky at that time of night.

In sloppy, drunken handwriting we shared the following exchange:

Me: I have to get up early tomorrow. I'll show you how to get to the Metro.

Him: Ok. What's your name again?

Me: Jana. Where do you need to get to tomorrow?

Him: School.

Me: Where's that?

Him: Gallaudet. Red line. Bed?

I appreciated his directness as my eyelids began to droop. He stood and grabbed my hand, and for a moment I thought about how strong and nimble his fingers must be, as they were his sole source of communication. I pictured him reading my body like a braille Kama Sutra.

There was, of course, doubt in my mind. But I had brought him home for a reason, and his being deaf didn't change that. If anything, my curiosity won out. I hoped his inability to hear would somehow make him better in bed—instead of having a heightened sense of smell, maybe he had a heightened sense of how to please a woman. And with that, I led him to my room.

However, it turns out that drunken sex with a deaf guy is extremely difficult. As I struggled to tug my meaty calves out of my jeans I knocked him onto my bed. It took him a moment to right himself and find his balance so he, too, could undress. He stood before me naked—a chest full of thick red hair and a constellation of freckles, his paleness emphasized by the harsh yellow living room light streaking in through my open bedroom door.

With the sound of sirens wailing somewhere in the distance, we attempted to recreate the lust that had gotten us there in the first place. I pushed him backward onto my bed, with purpose this time, and attempted a blow job. But the room was spinning and I couldn't interpret the noises he made. *Was he enjoying himself? Did he want me to stop?*

We switched positions and he pulled my legs around him. Unfortunately, once we got started there was no way to easily convey how unpleasant I found his shallow, mechanical thrusts. He couldn't hear my intermittent cries of "Oh, stop." And he mistook my grimaces of discomfort for cries of pleasure and just kept right at it. After several minutes of contorting my body to try to make it work, I finally tapped him on the shoulder, pulled myself free, and mouthed the words, "I'm tired. Sleep." After which I immediately turned my back to him and pretended to pass out.

At first light, I grabbed the pen and paper from the notebook on my nightstand and began sketching a map back to the Metro station. *How did I get here?*

Five months later, I was sitting in the living room perusing my Facebook newsfeed for important social networking nuggets when the little red bubble appeared, indicating a new message. I clicked over but didn't recognize the name of the messenger.

The body of the message simply said, "Hey, wanna fuck?"

The thumbnail picture of the sender did little to reveal his identity, though it appeared that this person was somehow one of my Facebook friends. Being the amateur detective that I am (I watch a lot of *Law & Order*), I opened the sender's profile to collect some personal information. His profile picture was a group shot from afar, but listed in his details was a notable point: he attended Gallaudet University, the leading university in the US for deaf and hard of hearing students. While on my computer that night several months earlier, Deaf Guy had apparently sent himself a friend request from my account. I was about to close his profile and ignore his message when I noticed another interesting tidbit: the link to his TheKnot.com page.

In another tab, I opened TheKnot.com—a wedding planning website I was familiar with from several friends' recent nuptials—and was bombarded with pictures of wedding cakes and happy couples, along with a wedding planning checklist. On the right-hand side of the homepage was a "Couple Finder." I entered Deaf Guy's name—gleaned from his Facebook page—in the search field. It yielded one result, a page which laid out all the details of his engagement and impending wedding to a deaf woman he met while attending Gallaudet. A picture of the couple, smiling happily at one another, was the focal point of their page. And underneath, their story. They had met three years earlier in a poli-sci class and had been engaged for almost a year.

It hit me hard. I was the other woman. This guy had cheated—or at least attempted to cheat—on his fiancée with me. And he was trying to do it again.

I clicked back over to his Facebook profile, still open in another tab. I had a second message waiting for me, even more succinct. "Wanna fuck?"

"Maybe you should ask your fiancée first," I typed in reply.

He unfriended me immediately. I never heard from him again.

THANK YOU, HPV

A consummate romantic, I had spent my college years sober and dateless, waiting for love to find me. I knew it would—Disney had told me so. No apple-induced coma or evil genie would deny me my prince. But, as naïve as I was, I wasn't blind. I had watched as the sloppy, drunken hookups around me blossomed into sloppy, drunken relationships. So, in late 2003, I decided to end my college career at Boston University with a bang. Finally feeling adult-ish, I succumbed to the flirtations of a mildly attractive man eleven years my senior with whom I regularly volunteered. This guy clearly had his shit together as evidenced by the fact that he didn't have roommates nor did he eat in a dorm cafeteria. He even had a full-time job.

I was so excited about my first real adult relationship that it didn't matter to me that this man was still excessively bitter about a divorce long in the past, that he constantly reminded me we weren't actually dating, or that he openly spoke about other women he slept with to push my buttons. I genuinely believed I was mature enough to handle a consensual, casual relationship. Unwittingly, I had fallen into the trap of naïve, fairy tale-loving women everywhere: I thought I could change him.

As anyone but me could have predicted, this man didn't change. Still, I was invested. I spent my weekends pretending his complete disregard for my feelings was quirky and fun, that I was easy-going and confident enough to handle it. I wasn't. But I thought if I could be, or at least pretend to be, he'd eventually let down his guard, open up to me, and, give up the consequence-free sex with the other women he was seeing.

One evening we were shooting pool at our usual spot—Boston Beerworks near the North End neighborhood. After he finished flirting with the waitress, a tactic he claimed to use to get better service, he put his cue down across the green felt table and unloaded on me. "You're too bland." "You're too indecisive." "Why don't you ever have opinions about anything?" It didn't feel like criticism. It felt like concern. He was finally opening up to me, or so I decided.

I thought I was making headway, chiseling away at his asshole façade when, in early 2004, I discovered he had infected a friend of mine with HPV. After my own Pap smear came back negative and my relationship with my friend had fractured, I finally gave up on changing the man and decided to change myself.

Having been a wallflower my whole life, my acceptance to George Washington University's School of Public Health and Health Services in Washington, DC offered the perfect opportunity to start anew. With a clean bill of health and HPV Guy's "thoughtful" critiques of my personality fresh in my mind, I moved to DC excited to start a whole new life with a brand new identity. I was tired of being typecast as the sarcastic-but-quiet sidekick who always followed the rules. I was ready to audition for the role of Unnamed Party Girl #1.

That August I moved to DC and adopted the method acting approach to my new life, accepting every social invitation that came my way. My new friends and I quickly settled into a routine of drinking-related activities every Thursday through Saturday. The part required a familiarity with alcohol, a substance I hadn't experimented with in my previous straight-edged life. But I was dedicated to my new persona and decided to give it a try. We became fast friends.

Just a few months into my first semester I was nailing the role. I was fun! Charming! Inebriated! I compensated for my social inexperience with unbridled enthusiasm. As I became more comfortable with my new outgoing personality, I used every opportunity to raise my visibility so destiny's GPS could find me amongst DC's urban clutter. More often than not, my friends would have to peel me off the face of a stranger at last call, or share an uncomfortable Metro ride with me and whatever new acquaintance I decided to bring home. I had no idea what I was doing, but I sure loved doing it. And I owed it all to HPV.

WHAT ARE FRIENDS FOR?

Following my one-night stand with the engaged Deaf Guy, I began to curb my drinking and sexual experimentation. I was starting to feel more confident in my social skills without the crutch of a cocktail. And, recognizing that my party girl character needed layers, I began to follow the lead of my friends who could imbibe all weekend without getting trashed every night. I wish I could say my behavior toward men improved as I toned down my drinking. It did not.

I was out with friends in Adams Morgan, a small neighborhood in Northwest DC full of bars and clubs of every ilk, one Saturday evening. We made a beeline for our favorite club, Heaven & Hell, ready for a night of dancing. It was early and the dance floor wasn't yet crowded, so I surveyed the bar. Almost immediately I exchanged glances with a cute guy and began my approach.

"Can I buy you a drink?" I asked. Though guys consistently reacted poorly to me offering to buy them a drink—perhaps because they felt it wasn't feminine, or, more likely because they just didn't want to engage with a shit-faced twenty-two-year-old—it was the only pick-up line I knew. This guy, however, accepted my offer, and shortly thereafter we were grinding on the dance floor.

At the end of the night as the lights came on for last call, my friends found us by the coat check making out. As they gently tried to pry me from his arms, my new friend Andres pulled me back to him and traced the deep V of my halter top with his tongue. While my friends stood there frozen with disgust, Andres and I exchanged numbers. I was feeling pretty good about myself for not sleeping with Andres that night. I assumed that meant I was developing standards.

When Andres called later that week to ask me out on a real date, something I had very little experience with, I congratulated myself on finally landing the guy. My experiences with dating were almost exclusively second-hand or movie-based; everything I knew about falling in love boiled down to four easy steps: 1) catch a stranger's eye across a room, 2) make him chase you, 3) some unclear things in the middle, and 4) live happily ever after. I was halfway there!

With exceedingly high expectations, I met Andres later that week in Dupont Circle, an eclectic but expensive area of DC. I couldn't really remember what he looked like, owing to the drinks and dim club lighting of our first encounter, so I was pleasantly surprised when he arrived. He was pretty cute. His light brown hair was neatly combed and though his attire was casual—a red T-shirt mostly concealing a thin gold chain around his neck, and baggy jeans—he walked toward me with confidence.

Restaurants and bars of every variety and price range

surrounded us, full of young, fresh-looking twenty- and thirty-somethings chatting about their day over glasses of wine. Overwhelmed by options, or perhaps just absent of thought, Andres couldn't decide where he wanted to eat. We walked up and down Connecticut Avenue in the heart of the upscale neighborhood, reading off each restaurant's name and speculating about the food within. "Why don't we try this," he finally announced as he held open a door and ushered me inside a Chipotle nestled between two day spas. I walked through the door and blinked as I waited for my eyes to adjust to the fluorescent lights overhead. Standing just inside the door, I surveyed the sad assortment of people silently eating burritos out of plastic baskets. *Ok, so he's not the romance-by-candlelight-type*, I thought. *Still, he's likely to woo me in some other yet-to-be-determined way.* I felt the self-assurance of someone who knows absolutely nothing about dating.

Dinner was nothing special. We engaged in chit chat as the salsa from his burrito poured down his hands, half the steak from his meal splattering out onto the table. But he asked me out again, and I just knew the second date would be better. I mean, it kind of had to be.

Somehow the next few dates were equally unimpressive. Conversation was superficial as we found we didn't have much in common. Still, I wasn't a quitter. We met, he gave chase (or at least called a few times) and now we were embarking on Step 3. This step, the movies had taught me, required time, effort, and, often some sort of setback accompanied by a catchy musical number. So, even though I wasn't exactly interested, when Andres invited me to his place to watch a movie for our fifth date, I felt renewed hope. Maybe we would find the chemistry we'd been lacking since our make-out session on the dance floor.

"What would you like to watch?" he asked that night, his hand already on my thigh. I surveyed his sparse collection of DVDs as he called out suggestions. I wasn't sure why he had so many romantic comedies, but I vetoed them all.

"Oooh, let's watch this." I stood and grabbed *Batman Returns* from the shelf.

"Are you sure?"

I knew what he was thinking, that *Batman Returns* wouldn't set the mood the way his more romantic suggestions would. But he didn't know me, or my love of Michael Keaton. Batman was sexier than any Hugh Grant character would ever be.

It didn't matter what movie we selected anyway. Ten minutes in, we were making out. But unlike on the dance floor, this time something caught my attention. Something was seriously wrong with his breath. Not oniony or garlicky—more like something was decaying in his mouth. I tried taking big gulps of air before going in, but I couldn't handle the stench. A few minutes in, I excused myself to use the bathroom where I conducted a desperate search for something, anything I could dab under my nose to mask the odor. Like Vicks VapoRub. Or gasoline. As I performed my search, I noticed something disheartening: a liter-sized jug of prescription mouthwash sitting on his bathroom counter. This wasn't just poor hygiene. This was a medical condition that modern science was powerless to fight.

Having found nothing of use to mask the odor, I walked back out to the couch defeated. Oswald Cobblepot and Catwoman hadn't yet forged their alliance against Batman; there was still a whole lot of movie left to watch. I was too polite and awkward to suddenly excuse myself from a date we had arranged days in advance. I knew he'd question my departure and I'd be unable to lie convincingly. So, as Andres moved back into position and the whiff of rotten fish à la dumpster settled around me, I knew what I had to do. As Oswald planned his campaign for Mayor of Gotham, I removed my shirt. This had the intended effect of diverting Andres's breath away from my face as he focused on my chest. Plus, it had the added bonus of allowing me to finish watching the movie undisturbed.

At this point, knowing that I had no intellectual or physical interest in Andres, it would have made sense to break up with him. But again, outside of high school, my dating skills had never really been tested. I didn't know how to break up with him, and he only pursued me harder after our movie date. I guess taking my shirt off had given him the wrong idea. I hated uncomfortable situations, and I really didn't want to hurt him. I rehearsed my breakup speech in the shower several times, but every time he called panic set in and I chickened out. So, we kept dating.

I decided to fall back on the tried and true method of cowards everywhere: get him to break up with me. So, each weekend when he called to invite me out I declined, explaining I had a ton of schoolwork to catch up on. Though true, I never actually stayed in on the weekends to study, as my grades could attest. I hoped Andres would feel neglected enough to cut me loose. This method backfired. Somehow, it seemed that no matter where my friends and I ended up on a Saturday night, we'd run into Andres.

Perhaps he had tagged me with a GPS locator when I wasn't paying attention, or maybe I just had terrible luck. But rather than take these opportunities to tell Andres we were over, I just ended up feeling guilty and consoling him with empty words about how much I liked him.

I was the worst and I knew it. So, I fell back on Plan B. I figured it would be easier to break up with Andres if I could help him find someone else on whom to focus his interest. My good friend and partner-in-crime, Ainsley, immediately came to mind. She was fun, flirtatious, and cute—tall with wavy blonde hair and bright blue eyes.

The next week I invited Andres to a party that Ainsley and I were both attending. I introduced them, pointed out all their similarities, put drinks in their hands, and left them to chat. I was a genius! Andres was none the wiser. Unfortunately, Ainsley was a smart cookie and very quickly called me out on my scheme.

"Just play along," I cajoled. "Let him see there are other great fish in the sea."

Though she had no interest in dating Andres—after all, I had told her about his breath and his overall lack of personality or appeal—she was always there for me in my hour of need. She agreed to help me out and went to work charming Andres. He left the party with her number.

Success! I thought as I rode the Metro home that night, proud of my ingenuity. I didn't know how Ainsley would handle it when Andres asked her out, but I knew that unlike me, she had no problem saying "No" when she wasn't interested.

I was walking home from the Metro station when my phone rang. It was Ainsley.

"Hey there!" I answered. "Thanks again for flirting

with Andres. You really saved me."

"Speaking of Andres, guess who just called me?" She sounded coy. Or drunk. Probably drunk.

"Already?" I was thrilled. "And?"

"He called to find out about you, if you actually like him." *Damnit!* "I told him I was still on the Metro and could barely hear him, so I'd call him back in a few. How would you like me to respond?"

It felt like I was back in sixth grade when my best friend Allison had called Seth Calvert to ask him if he liked me. I guess I still wasn't comfortable enough to do the dirty work myself, and three-way calling didn't feel like the way to go here.

Had I known about ghosting at the time, and been a much bigger bitch, my dating life might have taken a much different turn. Instead, I replied, "No. Tell him I don't. I don't want to see him anymore." I felt free, knowing that Ainsley would deliver the message.

"Ok. Just so you know, the first breakup is free. After that, I start charging." I couldn't tell if she was joking.

POLITICAL DIVIDE

Thoroughly disappointed that my relationship with Andres hadn't worked out the way all movies implied it would, I decided it was time to be a little more proactive about finding an appropriate suitor. I was familiar with the concept of online dating; however, given that it was 2005, my online options were limited. Dating apps like Tinder and OkCupid didn't exist yet, and there was still a financial cost and a social stigma associated with the few existing dating sites like eharmony and Match.

So I turned to the most reliable free site I could think of: Craigslist. I had acquired some great, if slightly damaged furniture there. I assumed it would work the same for boyfriends.

Almost immediately, I came across the dating profile of a guy named Everett who seemed well-spoken, funny, and able to quote *The Simpsons*. We started chatting, and within a week we met up for our first date.

Some notable things I learned about Everett during those first few dates: he had no breath (or other) odor issues, he was a staunch Republican, and he was a virgin.

He told me he was waiting for the right girl. I admired his willingness to forego casual sex for something more meaningful, and his sense of humor initially allowed me to overlook his sometimes in-your-face conservative ideals.

Unfortunately, a month into the relationship, I realized I was more okay than I should have been with our limited sexual contact. A full foot taller than me at six foot five, Everett was extremely thin, presenting as a stereotypical nerd, lacking in both sex appeal and confidence. And his outspoken political views were beginning to wear on me. During one date, as we walked through Metro Center station together, I stopped to admire artwork that had been hung to spruce up the otherwise drab cement station tunnel. Dozens of crayoned pictures by children from a local elementary school adorned the wall, depicting flowers and rainbows and other indecipherable objects drawn by young children who hadn't yet mastered their fine motor skills.

"That's really cute," I said, more to myself than to Everett.

"Sure, but it's not gonna help us win the war," he said, referring to the Iraq War, which, at the time, the US had been fighting for two years. He sounded annoyed that our youth were spending time exploring their imaginations rather than reciting the Constitution and stockpiling weapons.

I chose to ignore the comment, as I did with most of the political opinions he expressed. But it was becoming more and more difficult to hold my tongue.

A week later I was instant messaging with Everett when I should have been studying. He lauded then-President Bush, attributing the recent drop in unemployment to W's ingenious economic policies. I couldn't stay silent any longer. I registered my disagreement, pointing out that the drop in unemployment didn't correspond with an increase in the employment rate, and surmising a good chunk of the drop was from people giving up their job search altogether out of frustration. He quickly dismissed me as uninformed.

I was a little put off by his cursory rejection of my opinion, but I recognized that my understanding of most political topics was superficial at best, gleaned from write-ups in DC's free newspaper, *Express*, or from whichever news network happened to be on TV in the GW student center where I sometimes studied. Everett was pursuing his Master's degree in Government and Political Science, so I didn't push the issue.

The next week, however, we got into it again, this time over abortion rights. I may know next to nothing about economic policies, but a woman's right to choose was my hot-button issue, and one I was very knowledgeable about.

"I'm just saying, the day women truly take responsibility for their actions is the day we won't even need to debate abortion," Everett messaged me.

"Are you fucking kidding?!" I yelled at my computer. "What person under the age of eighty thinks like that?"

Instead, I typed, "Why is all the responsibility on the woman? If you and I have sex tomorrow and I get pregnant, why am I the one at fault?"

Backing away from that controversial comment, he approached his attack from a different angle. He next asserted that abortion caused pain and suffering to the fetus, another statement I vehemently refuted. A biology major in college, and a science nerd well before that, I could talk circles around Everett about topics related to physiology and fetal development. He wasn't used to facing such pointed opposition from me, and he quickly ended the discussion. Having grown up and gone to college in New England, I had never had to defend my pro-choice beliefs. I believed that angry old men were the only ones spouting anti-choice rhetoric, and that the issue would be resolved when they all died off. It was unnerving to know someone young and educated could align with that ideology.

Still, when he wasn't belittling my opinions or spouting repellent ideologies, things were good between Everett and me. My time with him didn't fill me with excitement, but I also didn't hate it. For the time being, that was good enough. Aside from Andres and a gay guy I dated back in high school, I didn't have a ton of real dating experience under my belt. It was becoming clear that I wasn't ever going to fall for Everett, but I viewed him as a Starter Boyfriend. I hoped things would work out between us, but if they didn't, at least I'd have more experience to add to my dating resume.

And then one evening, shortly before our relationship hit the two-month mark, Everett came over grinning from ear to ear.

Kat, my roommate, was home, so I pulled Everett into my room. "You seem happy," I said, kissing him hello. "What's up?"

He reached into his pocket and produced a condom. He walked over to my nightstand, opened the top drawer, and tucked the condom inside. "Tonight's the night." His eyes were brimming with excitement.

Had he not produced that condom, I probably could have kept dating Everett for months—he was smart and funny, wooed me often with flowers and compliments, and only offended me about half the time. But everything had just changed. I knew Everett had been saving himself, waiting till he found someone he really cared about before he had sex for the first time. I, on the other hand, could barely muster up more than lukewarm feelings for him. I couldn't be the one to take his virginity. As a woman, after all, I had to take responsibility for my sexual actions. So I'd have to break up with him.

Since Ainsley wasn't there to do it for me, I resigned myself to the fact that I'd have to crush his virgin heart myself. Only, I didn't know how. I should have done it right then and there, in my apartment. But instead, ten minutes later we were in his car driving out to a restaurant he wanted to try in the suburbs of Virginia.

He was chatty, almost manic, during the drive, experiencing the glee of a guy who knows he's about to get laid for the very first time. I sat silent, staring out the car window thinking about the nicest way to let him down. By the time we ordered our meals, my palms were sweaty and I was sick to my stomach. *I can't do it. He's so happy.*

I excused myself to the bathroom, where I dabbed myself dry. *You have to do it tonight*, I thought as I stared at my pale reflection in the mirror over the sink. *Do it quick and it's over. Do it. Do it. Do it.*

In that moment, I found my courage. I knew if I wavered even for a second, I might not be able to go through with it. I'd end up having sex with him and feeling like such a jerk that I'd probably just marry him rather than tell him the experience meant nothing to me. I nervously sat back down at the table across from Everett and told him I wanted to break up.

He stared at me, stunned into silence; I felt relief. And then the waitress came by to ask if I wanted a refill on my soda. "Your food should be right out." My momentary respite turned into panic as I was reminded that not only had we not yet received our food, but that we were out in the suburbs, miles away from the nearest Metro station. I needed Everett to drive me the twenty-five minutes back to my apartment.

We sat there in awkward silence, me staring down at my hands and glancing up occasionally to see Everett staring right through me, trying to piece together what had gone wrong and realizing that he would remain a virgin for the foreseeable future. I requested that the waitress wrap up our food to go and then quickly paid the bill.

"I'm assuming you need a ride?" Everett's voice sounded far away.

"Yeah. I think there's a Metro station about fifteen minutes from here." He nodded and I followed him to his car. I mentally prepared myself for what I assumed would be the longest fifteen minutes of my life. Yet instead of more silence, once settled in the car, Everett began rapid-firing questions at me. Why was I breaking up with him? Was there something he could do differently? When did I know it was over? Could we still be friends?

I did my best to be gentle with my answers, but he wasn't satisfied. Fifteen minutes later, he pulled into the Kiss & Ride lot—the DC area's sickeningly sweet euphemism for short-term drop-off lots around the region—at a Metro station on the Orange Line. "Is this ok? I can take you home if you'd prefer." It was an incredibly generous offer given the circumstances, but I couldn't bear another ten minutes in the car with his sad eyes and million questions.

"No, but thanks. This is perfect." I quickly exited the car and lied that we'd remain friends. I watched him drive out of sight from the station platform then ran up the towering escalator steps, desperate to get away in case Everett decided to circle back. Once safely seated on the train I let out a huge sigh of relief.

Breakups were harder than I had anticipated. Perhaps I needed to keep Ainsley on retainer.

REALIGNMENT

Fresh off of another relationship letdown, I threw myself back into the dating scene hard. I spent the summer going through men like I went through Chinese take-out—my preferred weekend hangover food. There was Rich, the nurse who liked to bite; Irish, the guy who spent more time curating the playlist to which we'd have sex than we spent actually having sex; Lars, the Swedish tourist on whom I blacked out in flagrante delicto; and an assortment of random men I made out with in bars because I liked their hats or their names.

"We maybe need to stop putting ourselves in these situations." Ainsley and I, and our two mutual friends, Jess and Angela, were all in agreement. "We've been lucky so far, but sleeping with random guys is dangerous," Ainsley said, continuing her assessment of our collective dating lives. It was late summer and our grad school course load hadn't yet picked up, allowing us time each evening to enjoy the city's happy hour scene. We were gathered atop The Reef, a three-story aquarium-themed bar in the heart of Adams Morgan, making the most of the fading warmth and sunlight.

Jess, a sweet, petite, extremely likeable girl from Nashville, attended grad school at GW with me and Ainsley. Angela, also petite with captivating brown eyes and a more forceful personality, was Jess's roommate and the unofficial social director of our group. It was one of those rare moments when all four of us were single at the same time. Though Jess and Angela had both been in serious relationships during the past year, both were newly unattached and were quick to take Ainsley's and my lead in enjoying the lifestyle. I had briefly curbed some of my wilder habits while dating Andres and Everett, but Ainsley and I were still known for imbibing a little too much and getting a little too friendly with strangers.

I'm not entirely sure why—perhaps it was Ainsley's sobering words about the real dangers we could face or how unfulfilled I felt after a summer of casual hookups— but in that moment I felt I was ready to make a change. And, not wanting to lead our friends down a potential path of self-destruction, Ainsley soundly proposed that we look out for one another so as to never end up in a potentially dangerous situation with a stranger. The four of us toasted, promised to keep an eye on one another, and ordered another round.

When the sun went down several hours later and the people on 18th Street—Adams Morgan's main strip—began to resemble less the buttoned-up Ann Taylor Loft models and more the Forever 21 pixies, the four of us decided to head over to Heaven & Hell to dance. It was still early and the bar was empty, so we ordered shots and took to the dance floor before it got too crowded.

Shortly after our arrival Jess and Angela were chatting up two guys at the bar while they waited for their drinks, and Ainsley and I made fast friends with two men standing off to the side of the dance floor. A week earlier, I probably would have invited one home with me, but the allure of awkward, fumbling sex with a stranger had lost its luster. Still, I was always up for a public make-out session and some light fondling. An hour and a half later when Jess and Angela came to inform us they were leaving, they found Ainsley and me at the back of the bar making out with our respective partners.

Ainsley and I extracted ourselves from our men and hugged our friends goodbye then stealthily reassessed our make-out partners for attractiveness. Catching each other's eyes, we decided to play it safe and head home as well. We grabbed our jackets, which had been stuffed in the back corner behind a fuzzy purple couch for safekeeping, and headed downstairs and out into the brisk evening air.

By then, 18th Street was a jumble of college and grad school students clad in tight tops and tighter pants, exhibiting various states of inebriation. The smell of pizza, sold in "jumbo slices" the size of three regular slices, wafted from small generic storefronts that blasted pop music and were nestled between bars. Cabbies, used to the unpredictability of late-night bar-goers, navigated the street deftly.

I briefly debated grabbing a jumbo slice to go but opted to wait and place my usual late night Chinese order when I got home. I had walked a half block up the road, lost in thoughts of sesame chicken and crab Rangoon, then turned to ask Ainsley if she wanted to grab a cab or walk back to the Metro together. Only, when I turned around, she wasn't there. Knowing she couldn't have gone far in the minute since I last saw her, I scanned the area immediately in front of Heaven & Hell, and that's when I saw her about to get into a cab with two men I'd never seen before.

"Ainsley!" I yelled as I ran to the cab. "Who are these guys?"

"They're chiropractors," she replied as if that answered my question. "I'm going to their hotel."

Rather than argue with her—my mind was functioning far too slowly for that after my evening of drinking—I jumped in the back seat next to Ainsley, and we were on our way toward L'Enfant Plaza, a business area in downtown DC near the Smithsonian museums.

"So, why exactly are we in a cab with these men?" I whispered to Ainsley, despite being two feet from either guy.

"I was trying to zip up my jacket, and I couldn't get it closed. This one"—she motioned to the guy sitting in the front seat—"came over and offered to help. He and his friends are in town for a chiropractor convention. They invited me back to their hotel to hang out." So much for making good decisions.

We pulled up outside the hotel in the heart of L'Enfant Plaza and immediately paired off—Ainsley with the guy who had resolved her zipper crisis, and me with what can only be described as the other one. Both men were average looking—moderate build, average height, short brown hair, wearing business attire. After an uncomfortably silent elevator ride, they took us on a strange tour of their hotel floor, perhaps looking for friends to party with. But, rather than a rowdy mob of drunken chiropractors, we came upon several rooms with the doors propped open, their occupants passed out on the beds within. Conversation between the four of us was limited and hushed to keep from waking those we had barged in on, so when we finally arrived at their own room I still knew almost nothing about these men.

I had already decided I wasn't going to sleep with my chiropractor; he was neither particularly attractive nor noticeably interesting. But I also wasn't about to leave Ainsley all alone. So I gave my chiropractor the green light to start feeling me up. This continued pleasantly for several minutes, but I became very aware of Ainsley and her chiropractor on the opposite bed just a few feet away. They were seriously getting into it, which simultaneously turned me off and my chiropractor on. He reached for the button on my pants, and I pulled away.

"I'm sorry, I'm really not feeling this," I said honestly. "I'm not interested in having sex tonight."

He was visibly annoyed that he got stuck with the prudish friend while his buddy was getting laid, and he grumpily asked me to leave. "I'm not going without my friend." I pointed at Ainsley, who was clearly enjoying herself and oblivious to my presence.

"Well, you're not staying here." My chiropractor got up and opened the door, motioning me out.

"Ainsley, I'm gonna be in the hallway, right outside this door," I said loudly enough that I hoped it would register. "If you need anything, or just wanna get out of here, I'll be right here." I made eye contact with my annoyed chiropractor in an attempt to drive home how serious I was.

"You're not closing this door on me," I told my escort as he led me out. I took my balled-up jacket and placed it on the floor in the doorway as I drunkenly lowered myself to the red and gold fleur-de-lis patterned hallway carpet. He rolled his eyes, clearly done with me, and left the door ajar as he headed toward the bathroom to shower and/or jerk off.

For the next ten minutes I sat on the floor just outside the chiropractors' room. Occasionally I peered in to ensure that Ainsley and her partner were still conscious and occupied, and that their third wheel wasn't trying to insert himself, so to speak.

When Ainsley finally walked out of the room, she smiled at me and asked if there was a cab stand out front. We barely spoke as we headed down to the lobby. The "safety pact" clearly needed some reinforcement, seeing as how Ainsley had forgotten the words she had spoken mere hours before. That would be a conversation best left for another time; we were both anxious to get home and wash the night off of us.

Once outside, we shared a laugh, hugged goodbye, got into separate cabs, and headed home as if it was just another night. Which, sadly for us, it sort of was. As the city blurred past me from the back seat of my cab, I knew I should have felt satisfied with how the night had turned out. I had been drinking for hours without getting trashed. I had successfully stuck with my friend to keep her safe. And, most importantly, I had been in the hotel room of a very willing, if prosaic, partner, and I had decided not to have sex with him. It was a huge step for me. One I should have felt proud of. Instead, I felt conflicted. I really had no desire to have sex with my chiropractor, but I felt I had missed out on an opportunity, another anecdote that would make me interesting and add to the lore of the exciting character I had created for myself. Without the drinking, the flirting, the random sexual encounters, was I in danger of reverting back to the quiet, uneventful life I had shed?

I wasn't sure I wanted to go back; I wasn't sure how to move forward. All I knew in that moment was that I should probably teach Ainsley how to zip her coat.

FREEFALL

Over the next few months I waged an internal war with myself. I had succeeded in starting over fresh in a new city with a whole new personality. I had made some genuine friends, but my grades were slipping, my sleeping patterns had become erratic, and my dating life was more about conquest than connection.

Something deep inside of me was telling me to stop, screaming at me to realize how unfulfilled I was, begging me to make smarter, healthier decisions. And, sometimes, like at the hotel with the chiropractors, I would. But inevitably, my resolve would break and the next week I'd be frantic for a hookup, not out of desire, but out of fear of being average, or worse—not being noticed at all. After a year of pretending to be outgoing, spontaneous, and sexy, my true nature—the self-respecting, rule-abiding introvert within—was trying to assert herself. And I did everything I could to destroy her.

The stress of trying to balance my competing personalities while also maintaining my grades, crushing it at my part-time job as an admin assistant at GW, and keeping my karaoke setlist fresh, resulted in late-night binging on an almost daily basis. My treat of choice: family-size bags of Peanut Butter M&M's. I began to look forward to this treat daily. The anticipation alone was like a high; I let it build throughout the evening until each night, around 1 a.m., it reached its peak. Then I would open my dresser drawer, where I concealed my stash from visitors and handymen, sneaking just a few M&M's at a time. Initially, I savored them, relishing the mixture of sweet and salty on my tongue. Quickly this faded to mindlessness. I would shovel pieces in my mouth—several at a time—without thinking, without noticing the flavors or textures or even my own hunger cues. I ate myself into a blissful stupor—aware of nothing, free from all stress and responsibility—stopping only when I felt uncomfortably full. My arousal back to reality always brought with it feelings of intense revulsion and temporary self-assurances that that was the last time; tomorrow would be different. Then I would tuck what was left of the mostly empty bag back into my desk drawer, hidden away so I wouldn't be reminded of my shame. But like clockwork every evening, I succumbed to temptation, frenzied for my next fix.

At the same time, my late-night take-out orders nearly doubled, including tasty add-ons like lo mein, egg rolls, or extra entrees. You know, in case I got hungry while sleeping. Over the span of a few months, I gained twenty pounds. I was disgusted with myself and none of my clothes fit anymore. But it wasn't until late November of my second year of grad school, as I sat on my bathroom floor leaning over the toilet with my fingers down my throat, that I recognized I needed help.

Thankfully, as a student I was able to access a counselor through GW's Counseling Center for a minimal fee and began the uncomfortable process of confronting my compulsive overeating on a weekly basis. In my sessions, we rarely talked about food, delving instead into the issues triggering my unhealthy behavior. However, recognizing that my physical health was a more immediate concern than could be addressed by the once-a-week therapy process—I was still binging and rapidly gaining weight—my counselor suggested I also attend Overeaters Anonymous meetings. I spent Sunday evenings for the remainder of my grad school days sitting stoically on a folding chair in the shabby annex of a church in the heart of Dupont Circle. There I listened to the stories of people struggling with issues similar to or worse than my own, witnessed them give their burdens up to a higher power. I never once spoke.

As my grad school days ended in the spring of 2006, I felt like I was making headway in my counseling sessions, though I had gained a cumulative forty pounds since the beginning of my compulsive overeating the previous year. Still, my binging had lessened, I was using the school's gym on occasion, and I made no additional attempts at purging. Things seemed to be getting better.

My first job out of grad school brought me north, back to Boston, where I had spent my undergrad years. After taking my sweet time to get settled, I finally got around to searching for a replacement therapist. Unfortunately, since I was no longer a student, therapists, including the ones my GW counselor had referred me to, were expensive. Those who were covered by my insurance still had higher per-visit co-pays than I could afford on my

$36,000 a year lab tech salary. So I unwisely decided I was strong enough to deal with my overeating alone.

Having a set routine certainly helped, initially. I was no longer staying up till 3 a.m. and sleeping till 11 each morning. I still ate compulsively, but in slightly smaller quantities than before. Since I now had roommates, my binges were harder to conceal.

Outwardly, I probably seemed fine. Happy, even. I loved my new coworkers; I had a stylish, modern apartment with an exposed brick wall in Brookline—a beautiful, upscale neighborhood just outside of down-town—with roommates I actually liked. I was back in a city I loved, reconnecting with old friends and easily making new ones. I joined a softball team and started volunteering with NARAL Pro-Choice Massachusetts, an abortion and reproductive rights policy and advocacy group. Life was good. Or at least, it should have been. But inwardly I was struggling to maintain control.

I don't know when it started—the monologue running through my head pointing out how fat, weak, stupid, and pathetic I was. But those thoughts eventually took over, drowning out all else, eroding what was left of my self-esteem. I would come home after a day of smiling and laughing with colleagues, cheering on my team through a softball victory, and bonding with friends over drinks, only to crumple into a ball on my bedroom floor and cry while the voice in my head degraded me.

I lived my life in fear. Fear that at any moment my boss and colleagues would discover that I was a fraud, that I was actually too stupid and inept to do my job. Fear that my friends and family would collectively realize just how worthless I really was and abandon me, leaving me all alone like the garbage I was.

I made a few short-lived attempts at dating during those four years in Boston, but the voice in my head reminded me often that no one would ever find me attractive enough to date, special enough to love. I hated my body—the physical representation of my weakness—so much that I couldn't stand the thought of being naked around another person ever again anyway. I wanted to be invisible. So, I gave up on dating.

My health also worsened during this time. When my right knee began to bother me, I ended up in physical therapy. Though I was given numerous exercises to strengthen the surrounding muscles and tendons, my therapist told me there was nothing she could do about the underlying cause: I was too heavy. My joints couldn't handle the added stress of my rather sudden weight gain. My mother pleaded with me to start a gym program, eat healthier, anything to lose weight. Diabetes ran in our family, and she was genuinely scared that it was only a matter of time before I became a diabetic like my grandmother. Unfortunately, the more I was told to lose weight, the more out of control I felt and the louder the inner taunting became.

For years, I pretended. Pretended I was happy, normal, working to lose weight to appease my concerned family. Those closest to me could probably sense that something was off, that I had lost my pep. But I never told anyone how deeply I was hurting.

One afternoon, deep into my depression, I attended an info session about bariatric surgery. I hoped it would offer a quick fix, be the switch I could flip to make myself thin and happy again. But, the physicians leading the session kept reinforcing that the process took time and commitment from those undergoing the procedure. And, one of the MDs I spoke with afterward informed me, I wouldn't be covered by insurance because, aside from being obese, I was otherwise too healthy to need the surgery. I was in a weird gray space—too fat to naturally support my own body weight, but too healthy to merit surgical intervention or a reality show on TLC.

As I walked out of that meeting considering my limited options, something clicked. There was no quick fix, and apparently, I was still healthy enough to reverse the damage without surgically altering my body. At that moment I believed I could fix myself.

That night, my usual evening torment set in. The voice in my head was cycling through the familiar list of insults—telling me that if I was a stronger person I would never have let myself get so fat; that no matter how much charity work or volunteering I did, it would never make up for the fact that I was selfish, narcissistic even; that my friendships were insincere, based on my need for approval rather than a genuine desire to connect. I had heard it all before. Yet this time I sat up and stared at my red, puffy face in the mirror and somehow found the energy to fight back.

I'm a good person, I remember thinking to myself. I had been a volunteer EMT in high school, was certified by the Red Cross to teach CPR and first aid classes to help people learn lifesaving skills, and was currently doing what I could to help women access safe reproductive health and abortion services. I wasn't worthless. I cared about people. I truly did.

And I'm strong. I'm going to get healthy.

The voice continued its attack, but each night I found the strength to rebuff the insults. When it called me stupid, I reminded myself of my academic achievements—that I had graduated in the top 12 percent of my high school class, received several college scholarships, attended two highly respected universities, and landed a pretty decent first job where I was doing well with little-to-no supervision. When it called me unlovable, I remembered the wonderful friends and family I was fortunate to have, despite the most recent years when I had kept so many of them at arm's length.

As I grew stronger, the voice got weaker, until one day I no longer felt like crying. Instead, I threw out my hidden stash of candy. I enrolled at a gym down the street and began working out every day on my way home from work, seriously testing the limits of my gym short lycra. I began paying attention to portion sizes and even started seeing a nutritionist regularly.

Slowly—so very slowly—I began to turn things around. I don't know when it ended, but one day the derisive voice in my head was gone.

When the contract for my job in Boston ended in July 2010, I followed the money to the first job I could get, which happened to be in Atlanta. I was terrified of making the move, both because, as a fierce liberal I feared the close-mindedness I assumed I would experience in a solidly red state, and because I didn't know anyone in Georgia.

In retrospect, the move turned out to be the best possible thing for me at that time in my life. Not only was I dead wrong about my Southern stereotypes—the people I met in Atlanta were progressive and genuine and compassionate—but I was able to use my first few months with no social life to establish a healthy routine for myself. I came home from work every day and went to the gym, then prepared a home-cooked meal. I actually started losing weight and feeling positive about my body. Not just positive, but proud. The day I weighed myself and found out I had finally slimmed down from morbidly obese to obese (no modifier needed), I was ecstatic. And, with Krispy Kreme a mere two blocks from my apartment, I celebrated with a donut. The mere fact that I was able to limit myself to a single celebratory donut was testament enough to my achievement. No one in Atlanta knew how far I had come, but I was amazed by what my body was capable of and by the willpower I had found to keep it going. I still knew nothing about how to find love with a partner, but I was starting to learn how to love myself.

MANSPLAINED

As I became more confident in my body specifically, and myself more generally, I waded back into the dating pool during my two years in Atlanta, but I stumbled every time. In reality, I had lost out on at least four formative years when I should have been experiencing love and heartbreak and additional STI scares, years I should have been learning and maturing. Though I was fast approaching thirty, I was still a dating neophyte.

And while I enjoyed the people and the food (in moderation, of course) of Atlanta, my northern body couldn't adjust to the brutal heat, and my previously urban lifestyle was incompatible with the city's reliance on cars. So, in January 2012, I jumped at the opportunity to return to DC as a contractor for the National Institutes of Health (NIH).

I had loosely been making use of my grad degree—an MS in Public Health Microbiology & Emerging Infectious Diseases—over the years. I started as a microbiology lab tech in two Boston-area hospitals, and worked most recently as a public health researcher in Atlanta, developing health programs to address gaps in care for underserved populations. My new contractor gig would allow me to work with researchers to develop and refine tools and measurement systems used in cancer prevention, diagnosis, and treatment. Since reading Richard Preston's *The Hot Zone* and *The Cobra Event* in high school, I had wanted to study and prevent diseases in any way I could. The more contagious, the better. Though I would not be developing life-saving vaccines or tracking outbreaks in my position at the NIH, and cancer was generally a chronic noninfectious disease, I was excited about my new role as a disease researcher.

My office was located in White Flint, a neighborhood just north of Bethesda, Maryland, and about thirty minutes north of downtown DC via the Metro. Most of my grad school friends had moved away in the six years since I'd been gone, but my best friend Kat still lived in Arlington, Virginia. That was farther than I was willing to commute, so rather than search for a place near her, I hopped on Craigslist and found a room in a two-bedroom luxury condo just a fifteen-minute walk from work. The pictures of the unit and the building were beautiful, and the area itself seemed to have a lot going on. That month, after some conversations with the owner, I flew to DC to check out the condo with Kat—now a contracts lawyer for the federal government—to meet with the owner and sign the lease.

"It's a two bedroom, but I'm only renting out one of the rooms while I'm away," Ray, my soon-to-be landlord, and owner of the unit, was explaining. His wife, an attractive Colombian woman, judging from the pictures hanging throughout the apartment, was a doctor and had just been hired on to a year-long contract with the World Health Organization. She would be moving to Geneva for that year, so Ray was moving with her. He had quit his job as an analyst for a national consulting firm and was tasked with renting out the condo before flying out to meet her. Ray was bland in appearance and demeanor—short brown hair, average build and height, monotone voice with a Maryland accent that became apparent whenever he said "Warshington." But he was very accommodating and didn't seem overtly crazy.

"We'll keep our bedroom vacant so we have a place to stay when we return to the States for holidays and conferences. But basically, the place is yours. I'll continue to pay half of the utilities. I just really need to get this place rented in the next few days." I looked around at my new digs. While the bedroom had been euphemistically described as "cozy," I had my own bathroom and would have the run of the common areas, including the in-unit washer and dryer. Plus, the building had a nice gym and an outdoor pool. Sure, I was a minimum thirty-minute Metro ride to downtown DC, but the few friends I had left might visit if I enticed them with a pool party. It was a snowy January afternoon, but that gave me five months to get my social life in order.

Nervous that this housing agreement appeared too good to be true, I had Kat review the lease before I signed. Ray was leaving for Geneva in two days, but would be back the weekend I moved in to help me get settled.

"That guy seems really nice. And the condo is sweet. I can't believe I get a two bedroom condo all to myself!" I was clearly excited as I climbed into Kat's car and she pulled out into the poorly plowed Maryland streets.

Though it snowed in DC every winter, it still seemed to take the city and surrounding suburbs by surprise.

When something seems too good to be true, it usually is.

I arrived at my new home with two suitcases the last weekend in February, and, true to his word, Ray was there to meet me. The rest of my stuff was coming up via moving truck and hadn't yet arrived.

With minimal unpacking to do, I felt a little out of place in my new digs. My room was tiny, and I didn't yet have a TV or a desk on which to house my computer. I was staring out the window at the barren trees in the courtyard below, experiencing the typical pangs of loneliness I felt whenever I first moved to a new area, when Ray knocked on my door.

"Hey, I'm going back to Geneva in a few days, but I wanted to go over a few things with you." I followed him out to the living room to find the vacuum on the floor.

"I keep the vacuum in the laundry room." He pointed to the small room just off the dining area. "Let me show you how it works." He grabbed the cord and went to plug it into the wall.

A little surprised, I told him I knew how to use a vacuum. "Ahh, but this one is bagless," he explained, as if that made the process of vacuuming somehow different. He clearly wanted to make sure I knew how to use it, so I stood there slightly amused as he vacuumed the living room floor.

As the whirring stopped and he unplugged the vacuum from the wall, I assumed our little lesson was over. I was wrong.

"Now, when I come home I like to lock the door behind

me right away. That way I don't forget to do it later." He smiled at me and proceeded to demonstrate—opening the front door, walking outside, then stepping back inside, shutting the door, and locking it behind him. "You see, the doorknob has a lock, but we also have a deadbolt. Please make sure you lock *both* locks immediately when you come home."

I'm not sure if he thought for some reason that I was an idiot, or if he just spoke down to everyone, but I had survived my entire adult life living in major urban centers—including two years in an apartment building in a rough area of Atlanta—as a single woman. If I knew anything, it was how to lock a freaking door. But rather than interrupt his demonstration, I just smiled and nodded as if this was all a very new concept. *Two locks. Why had no one ever thought of that before?*

Thankfully, he was done patronizing me for the moment, so I retired to my room to finish settling in. I wanted to wash my sheets so there'd be a fresh clean bed to cozy into on my first night in my new home. It was amazing to have an in-unit washer and dryer, and I reminded myself how lucky I was to have found this apartment. The owner might be a bit peculiar, but he was leaving soon.

The next day, I stocked up on groceries and explored my new neighborhood. I was a twenty-minute walk from a shopping center that housed a Target and an Old Navy, both stores a thrifty girl like me enjoyed. I then did a test-walk of my route to work. It wasn't particularly scenic, but it was straightforward, following a major roadway past several office parks.

I returned home that evening to an empty apartment.

There on the kitchen table to greet me, was a pile of lint and a very long handwritten note. Ray had inspected the lint trap after I did laundry and was dissatisfied with how I left it. He very clearly thought that, though I had lived on my own for the past twelve years, I had never done my own laundry. Yes, I knew about cleaning out lint traps. I sometimes did it after completing a load of laundry, but more often I did it before starting a new load. The next time I put something in the dryer, I would have cleaned out the lint first. I guess that wasn't acceptable in this household, so I made a mental note and threw out the lint, along with the note.

I then preheated the oven for a frozen pizza I had bought for dinner and moved to the couch to decompress and watch some TV. Ray came home shortly after, making a show of locking both locks right behind him. He greeted me with a smile and made no mention of the missing pile of lint. As he unlocked his bedroom door (yes, he kept his bedroom door locked), he offhandedly said, "I'm glad you figured out how to use the oven. It's digital, so if you're used to knobs you might not get it."

I wanted so badly to scream, "I'm not a moron! I know how to perform basic human tasks!" But the beeping of the oven timer interrupted my internal cries. Instead, I pulled out my pizza and ate alone at the kitchen table, fuming. *Just a few more days*, I reminded myself. *He'll be gone in a few more days.*

When I finished my pizza, I went to wash my dishes at the sink and noticed that there was no drying rack on the counter. So, I opened the dishwasher and found it mostly full.

"Has this been run? Are these dishes clean?" I asked Ray, who was now on the couch flipping through the channels.

"Oh, they're always clean. We don't run the dishwasher. That's where we store the clean dishes." He returned to his channel-surfing.

I wasn't sure if he was using the royal "we" or not, but I washed my dishes and placed them in the dishwasher to dry. I then opened a few cabinets to see what, if not dishes, lived inside. They were half-filled with lots of useless pots and jars, most likely from places Ray and his wife had traveled. There was plenty of room for clean, dry dishes. But I didn't tell Ray that. I just quietly decided to clean out the dishwasher the following week, when it would be safe to do so.

At that point, Ray had settled on a channel. He was watching a soccer match in Spanish, despite the fact that he was born and raised in Annapolis, Maryland and his Colombian wife was in Switzerland. And, though he was sitting a mere seven feet away, he was blasting the match at a deafening volume. I snuck into my room, closed the door, and attempted to read despite the cheers and screaming fans in the next room.

I spent the next few days trying to avoid Ray. I also invested in a pair of earplugs, as it turned out his favorite activity was watching any and all Spanish programs, including telenovelas, at maximum volume. When I finally heard the door close behind him, followed by the familiar double-click of the locks, as he left for the airport, I said a silent prayer of thanks. I could finally let lint pile up, put the dishes away, watch English-speaking television at a moderate volume, and stare at the vacuum cleaner in wonderment without feeling judged. For four amazing months, I made that condo my own.

I spent those months establishing a healthy routine: walking to and from work, returning home to use the gym, then making myself a moderately healthy dinner. Since I no longer had a bustling social life, I was home much of the time enjoying my nice, spacious apartment.

Until one awful day in mid-May.

I returned from work one evening, walking down the main breezeway toward the condo with my headphones in. Despite my absorption in Iyaz's catchy "Replay," when I turned the corner to my hallway, I heard Spanish TV blaring. The closer I got to my door, the louder the Spanish. I braced myself for what was waiting for me inside, took a deep breath, then entered.

As if it was completely normal for him to be doing so, Ray was sitting on the couch watching the evening news in Spanish. He smiled and greeted me when I entered but made no effort to explain his sudden appearance. I moved quickly to my room, changed, and headed to the gym per my usual nightly routine. When I returned an hour later, he had neither moved nor adjusted the volume. I poured myself a glass of water and casually queried him about his presence.

"So, are you back for a conference? Is this going to be like a week-long thing?" I wasn't sure I could take a whole week of him.

"Oh, did I not tell you?" His eyes briefly met mine before returning to the TV. "I didn't like living in Switzerland. I actually got a new job here and decided to move back. We're gonna be roommates."

I almost choked on my water. *Roommates? For the remainder of my year-long lease? Could I get out of this? How had he "forgotten" to tell me he was moving back?*

Despite what was going through my mind—the anger, the shock, the escape plans I was hatching—I managed an utterance of congratulations and snuck off again to my room.

In the coming months, that tiny bedroom would serve as my only refuge. Ray's new job, it turned out, allowed him to work from home. Every. Day. And, condescension must have been his primary language, because he had no friends to speak of. So there he sat, in the living room all day, every day. When he wasn't working, the TV was on full blast, always in Spanish. And when I ventured into the kitchen to grab food, he would ambush me with conversation, always about something inane like the weather or public transportation infrastructure in major cities.

On the bright side (if you really spin it), my desire to avoid Ray spurred me toward self-improvement. Each evening, I would dash into the kitchen, fix myself something for dinner, and eat it in my room. If I forgot to grab salt or a knife or dessert, I had to make do without. I started losing weight because I didn't want to chance a trip to the kitchen and wind up in a forty-five-minute discussion about the pros and cons of dedicated bike lanes along Rockville Pike, the major road paralleling our building. I also spent more time at the gym just to escape my cubbyhole in the evenings. And, since I hated feeling trapped in the condo, I accelerated my search for a fulfilling social life to occupy my time. In retrospect, I should be thanking Ray. He mansplained me right into a social life.

THREE YEARS

Growing up, my mother used to tell my sister and I that we didn't need men in our lives to be happy. What mattered was that we were happy with ourselves. The words must have had an effect, since several of my earliest pieces of writing are follow-ups to the Cinderella story. In one, Cinderella realized she didn't, in fact, love the prince and wanted to move out. Since moving back in with her wicked stepfamily wasn't an option, she went out, got a job at Walmart, and saved enough money to build her own castle. Though prince-less, she was happy and in control of her own life. It was enough to bring tears to the eyes of feminists everywhere.

I vividly remember my mother telling me all about women she worked with who were in their forties and had never married. She assured me they lived completely happy, full lives. She brought this up, I assume, because at that time I was in my late-twenties and rarely discussed dating. The men I went out with didn't stay in my life long enough to be worth mentioning. At the time, it didn't bother me too much. I was still young and figuring things out. I had complete faith that it would just happen for me someday, as it had seemed to happen, almost effortlessly, for all of my friends, relatives, and social media contacts.

When discussing plans for my brother's wedding, and, a few years later, my sister's, my parents assured me that they had set money aside for me as well, in a condo fund. Though it seemed a little callous to have already resigned themselves to the fact that I'd never find someone, it was reassuring to know that my parents would never pressure me to be in a relationship or to get married. Don't get me wrong, I had always wanted the traditional life—to fall in love and to marry, as my siblings had. I wanted children, a family of my own. I wanted the house in the 'burbs with the spacious backyard where my husband and I could adoringly push our young children on the swing set. I truly did. But I was thankful there was no external pressure complicating my search.

And then I turned thirty.

My parents, both three years from retirement at that point, had already purchased a plot of land in a beach community in southern North Carolina. They were beginning to purge all clutter from their home in Connecticut and plan the next phase—the beach phase—of their lives.

We were all together at my cousin's wedding in Newark, Delaware, drinking, eating, and photo-boothing it up. I showed my dad how to dance to pop and hip-hop music, borrowing my instructions from DJ Kool. ("When I say freeze you just freeze one time. When I say freeze y'all stop on a dime.") When the cupcakes came out we stopped dancing briefly, retiring to our table with fresh drinks in hand and buttercream remnants stuck to our noses.

Looking around at our family and the others in attendance, my mom casually remarked, "This is so nice." Then, looking at me, "You know you've got three years to find someone to marry. Once your dad and I retire, we're not paying for a wedding." She said the words breezily, as if she was saying, "I'll have another Jameson on the rocks," which is exactly what I suddenly felt like saying. My mind was racing back to the many ways my mom had made sure not to pressure me, and then I realized it had all been a trick. She'd assumed that with no pressure from her, I'd find someone in college, like my sister had, or right after college like my brother. She fed me reassuring words, as all mothers do, never knowing she'd end up with a very independent, single thirty-year-old daughter on her hands. Her words had been platitudes, but they had worked too well and now she was trying to undo it all. After a certain age, Cinderella should just stay with the prince. At least she'd have a comfortable retirement and her Fairy Godmother could rest easy knowing that her job was done.

The clock was ticking.

Part 2

DELUSIONS AND DISAPPEARANCES

SOFTBALL

I joined the National Institute of Health's spring softball league shortly after my cousin's wedding, in April of 2012. Jared, the team coach, offered me a ride to the first game since I didn't have a car and the games were all played on community fields in the suburbs of Rockville, Maryland. We arrived a half hour early for our first game and, as we ascended the small hill to the field, I noticed one lone guy sitting on a bench, glove in hand. He stood and walked toward us.

"Jared?" he asked.

"Yep. You must be James. Nice to meet you." They shook hands, then James turned to me. I smiled, introduced myself, and shook his hand. I had found my new crush. In fact, my first crush in a while. He was tall and muscular, and, I quickly assessed, could easily support my body weight.

Jared began working on the lineup while James and I tossed the ball around. As we warmed up, I learned that he had moved to the DC area from Alaska the previous summer and had, years earlier, been in the Marine Corps.

Also, he had a great arm. Well, great arms. I was slightly disappointed when the rest of the team began arriving, intruding on our alone time. I guess we sort of needed them to play, but still.

The next week, Jared was away, traveling for work. I didn't know anyone else on the team well, so I sent out a general email asking if I could hitch a ride to the game. I pressed "Send" as I crossed my fingers that James would be the first to respond. He was. Within minutes of the initial message, he and I had agreed on a meeting time and place. As the weeks progressed, I sought rides from James and Jared on alternating weeks so as not to seem too eager for James's company. Subtlety is definitely not my strong suit, but if James knew how interested I was, he downplayed it marvelously.

As spring quickly turned into summer, I was loving my NIH team. Everyone was fun, friendly, and responsible. That could be owing to the fact that everyone on the team, with the exception of me and James, had or was in the process of acquiring a PhD, and most had spouses and children. There were no jocks, only nerds. Even our trash talk was highbrow: "Why don't you go publish a manuscript, or do something else that actually matters." Sick burn!

Unfortunately, that also meant that instead of hitting the bar after our games, my teammates had to rush home and tend to their families, cram for exams, and/or finish drafting those important manuscripts. So, by the end of June when we were halfway through the spring season, my relationship with James was still relegated to conversations in the front seat of his faded green pickup on the way to and from games, and occasional banter on the field. When the Fourth of July rolled around, I seized an opportunity to move things along.

Kat lived in a high-rise near the Potomac River in Arlington, Virginia. Her building's management company was throwing a Fourth of July party, complete with dinner, booze, live music, and dessert. She invited me and a few others to the party with the intention of heading to a park across the Potomac from the National Mall for the fireworks. It sounded perfect, and I knew James hadn't yet been in DC for the Fourth. I also knew, based on his insistence that he didn't have any friends (and that's the way he liked it), that he'd be free that night.

As I had hoped, James had no plans and agreed to accompany me to Kat's. It was perfect. I'd finally get to wear normal, non-sweat-wicking clothes around him. Plus, Kat could observe our interactions and report back that he liked me. I mean, *if* he liked me. But he did... Right?

I met James outside my building on the Fourth. I was wearing my favorite white capris and a violet wide-neck shirt that hid my untoned upper arms. I wore my hair down, and the July humidity added country music–style volume to my cascading curls. "You look nice," James greeted me. I knew it. He was practically in love with me!

Now, James wasn't the greatest conversationalist. He would answer direct questions, but almost never expounded without prodding. He also rarely turned the questions around to invite my responses. So, I spent much of the Metro ride to Kat's interviewing James and allowing his extremely blue eyes to convince me that we were sharing an amazing connection. Even while he was telling me that he hated the DC area and couldn't wait to move back to the Middle-of-Nowhere, Michigan, where he was originally from, I convinced myself that we still had a shot. His hobbies included shooting (alone), archery (alone), and generally just avoiding all the best parts of DC because they were too crowded. It was clear James wasn't interested in sharing his hobbies with me, or anyone else.

In truth, I enjoyed shooting. Years ago, a friend and I had been interested in target shooting. At the time, I was living in Boston, where gun laws were quite strict. So, we signed up for the eight-hour gun safety course, at the end of which we got to enter the range and shoot under the supervision of an instructor. It turned out I had a knack for it, and I found the act of shooting at a target quite soothing. I returned weekly to practice with my instructor and, once I was confident enough in my abilities, I applied for a license, which I received after passing a shooting exam and an incredibly thorough background check. Of course, the hard work I put into acquiring my gun license was rendered moot when I moved to Atlanta and the only requirement needed for a license was proof that I was a resident. But hell, how important is it really to know how to clean, hold, or aim a gun?

Our mutual enjoyment of shooting and softball were, however, the only areas of overlap in the Venn diagram of James's and my interests. Though also an introvert, I enjoyed living in the city and interacting with people regularly. In fact, half of the reason I still played softball was to meet new people and hopefully parlay those new relationships into friendships. Having moved around so much as an adult, I was becoming quite adept at insinuating myself into people's personal lives until they gave up and just accepted that I was part of their group.

But I wasn't going to let a little hatred of people and

cities and everything else that brought me pleasure get in between me and James and what could be extremely hot sex. While he continued listing the reasons he couldn't wait to get back to Michigan, I was imagining my legs wrapped around him.

We arrived at Kat's shortly after 6 p.m., but the "party" didn't exactly go as planned. The fireworks started at 9:15 p.m. according to the city website. At quarter of eight, none of Kat's other friends had yet arrived.

Finally, just after eight, Kat's somewhat socially awkward basketball teammate who lived down the street arrived...with three unexpected guests. Usually that wouldn't have been an issue, except they were all about as chatty as James. So there Kat and I sat in her apartment surrounded by mutes. Since Kat and I had known each other since middle school, and we were becoming heavily intoxicated, we took the lead as the in-house entertainment. While the others looked on quietly, Kat and I put on a two-person show.

"Remember that time we changed the words to 'Baby One More Time' and shot a music video for our final project in trig class?

...*My ignorance is killing me (and I)*

I must confess I still believe (still believe)

That when I'm graphing I lose my mind

Give me a sine

Hit me, cosine, one more time," I stupidly sang to the group.

"Haha, yep. We aced that project."

Surveying our silent audience, I added, "That would have been a lot more entertaining if you knew us in high school."

We babbled for what felt like hours but was, in

actuality, only about forty-five very painful minutes.

A little after nine, the last two guests finally arrived, and we began making our way downstairs. Unfortunately, when we stepped outside at 9:10 p.m., we heard the familiar boom of fireworks. The show had started earlier than expected. Instead of relaxing on blankets in the park—and me taking the chance to cozy up to James—we sped over to a fence lining the side of the highway and craned our necks to catch what little remained. I had promised James one of the best fireworks displays in the country (and possibly a reason to stay in DC). Instead, I delivered a semi-obstructed, distant view of half a fireworks show.

Afterward, our group walked back toward the Pentagon City Metro station to catch the train home. I attempted to make conversation with any and all present, but there were no takers. They were probably just tired from watching me talk all night.

James and I left the group when we switched to the Red Line at Gallery Place. He was quiet as we waited for our train. I made attempts to interview him as I had on the way to Kat's earlier that evening, but he was even more restricted in his responses, and I was exhausted from entertaining. After a few minutes of silence, James sullenly confided that he hated the Metro and the swarms of people who rode it. The swarms of people who currently surrounded us.

Now, most people don't look at an antisocial guy who has trouble making conversation and think, *He's totally boyfriend material.* But I was on a deadline, and again, he was extremely attractive.

Thirty minutes later, after a quiet and moderately

uncomfortable train ride back to Rockville, we parted ways in front of my apartment without so much as a hug. But I wasn't deterred.

Since my romantic Fourth of July hadn't exactly gone as planned, I decided to invite James to something a little more his speed. Kat and I had planned to kayak later that weekend anyway, so I invited him along. I was prepared for a nice relaxing trip along the Potomac, as my previous kayaking outings with Kat were more leisurely than athletic. And Kat, in a kind attempt to give me and James some alone time on the river, pulled out ahead of us and took off, putting distance between her boat and ours. But unexpectedly, James, clearly not wanting to be outdone, took off after her. Apparently, he was competitive. I spent the entire hour playing catch-up and churning up far too much of the Potomac in the process. I arrived back at the boathouse a solid ten minutes after them, sweating, sore, and covered in river water.

Our outing had yet again failed to live up to my expectations, so I decided it would be best to restrict our time together to softball-related activities. At least, until I could come up with a better plan to get him to like me.

"Wait. You don't believe in seatbelts?" James and I were seated in his truck waiting for others to arrive at the field one afternoon. "You mean you don't believe they exist, or you don't believe they save lives?" I was trying not to act too disturbed by what he had just said. After all, he was so pretty, and I had already invested a lot of time in this imaginary flirtation.

"I don't think they do anything. Sure, sometimes they save people, but sometimes they don't. A buddy of mine got hit head-on by another car a few years back. The steering column would have impaled him if he had been strapped in place by a seatbelt. Thankfully, he wasn't wearing one, and when his seat back broke, he was able to slide back and avoid the impact."

I was too hung up on his initial statement, "I don't believe in seatbelts," to point out that even with a seatbelt on, his friend would have been able to slide backward with the seat. Is it possible he didn't know what a seatbelt was?

"What if you came across one of those police traps where it's clear they're stopping cars just to make sure people are wearing their seatbelts? Would you at least buckle up to avoid a ticket?"

He didn't hesitate. "Nah. I'd take the ticket. I'm not gonna pretend I use seatbelts. That's stupid."

"*That's* stupid?" My voice was slightly raised, but I was able to keep the exasperation out of my tone. "Well, I guess if we get into a terrible accident and only one of us survives, we'll find out which of us was right."

He nodded, clearly as done with the conversation as I was. We changed topics to softball and began discussing our chances for a win based on how the team had been doing recently. We had knocked out all but the first and second place teams in the double-elimination tournament, but we also had a loss under our belts. Another loss today would end our season.

"How's the online dating been working out for you?" he suddenly asked. I had confided earlier in the season that I had been using the free dating site OkCupid for some time now, though mostly unsuccessfully. The question came out of nowhere, but I was encouraged that he showed an interest in what passed for my love life.

"It's alright. I had a date last week and have two more lined up for next week. I wouldn't say I'm terribly excited about either of them, but I'm still hopeful." I wanted to let him know that I was a sought-after commodity—at least to people I'd never met—while making it clear that I was still very single and looking. As an afterthought I added, "How about you? Anything exciting on the horizon?" In the months I had known him, he had gone on maybe two first dates with no success. While extremely attractive—blond hair, blue eyes, solid muscle—he preferred being alone to socializing, meaning that in the year since he had moved to Maryland, he had met very few people.

"Actually, yeah. I've been seeing someone for a few weeks." The words landed like a one-two punch. First, and most painfully, while I was laying months of groundwork with this guy, he was off seeing someone else. I had seen him at least once a week every week since April, and he had never brought this up. Did his mention of it now mean it was getting serious? Second, how had a socially awkward hermit managed a more successful dating life than me?

As I pulled myself out of my daze, I realized he was still talking. "She wants to go to this place that has belly dancing shows." He couldn't have sounded less excited about this girl.

Mustering my best genuinely enthusiastic voice, I said, "That sounds like fun. It's a really interesting date idea." Then, switching to my more reserved "I'm concerned" tone, I added, "You don't sound excited, though."

"Eh. It's probably going to be really loud and hard to have a conversation."

"Yes. And you get to watch attractive, scantily clad women dance around for you. I don't see the problem. Can't you just enjoy it as a fun activity that you didn't have to plan? You can talk after." I wasn't sure why I was trying to convince him to be open-minded. I should have been agreeing with him, discouraging him from even going on this date.

"I prefer to talk. I don't need to watch people dance." He could have fooled me. Conversing with him wasn't particularly easy. Sometimes he was full of things to say; other times it was like pulling teeth. Regardless of his mood, I generally had to initiate.

"On our last date we went to this place called Jaleo." He mispronounced it with a hard "J" though it was a Spanish tapas restaurant. "I think the food we had was called tapas..." He said the word slowly, awkwardly, as if the only ethnic food he was familiar with was pizza. "Everything was so weird. I tried it all, but... yuck."

I was familiar with Jaleo, and quite enjoyed their food. Who doesn't enjoy figs wrapped in bacon washed down with peach sangria? A monster, that's who.

"Can't you just take solace in the fact that you get to hang out with a girl you like? It shouldn't matter what you're doing if you really like her." I was now drawing on my experiences as an introverted college kid, more often than not being the comforting friend to guys I interested in, helping them attract or reconcile with girls who weren't me. My concern for his happiness sounded genuine. And the part of me that had already resigned myself to forever being his friend—and only his friend—

was sincere. The rest of me, including the part that wanted to get laid, was just phoning it in.

Thankfully, our teammates began to arrive, giving me a way out of the uncomfortable conversation. Before taking the field for practice, I texted Kat, *So James's been dating someone. I'm ALWAYS the friend.* And with that, I played my worst game of the season, contributing to our final loss, our team's ejection from the tournament, and the end of our softball season. It was the perfect time to take a break from James.

In retrospect, I'm not even sure how much I actually liked James. He was attractive for sure. But that was about it. Yet for some reason, it didn't matter to me that James and I had nothing in common, that we valued different lifestyles, that I believed in provable facts and statistics and he believed in hearsay and magic. At the time, all that mattered was getting him to like me.

Much like a seatbelt, I would never find myself wrapped around him. He was now free to hurtle through life's windshield without me.

ESCAPE TO NY

The dank, urine-scented bus terminal with its ever-present puddles of oil and (I hoped) water served as the perfect contrast to my mood. It was Friday morning, and I was boarding a bus for New York to meet up with Angela, who now lived in NYC, and Ainsley, who was there interviewing for a job. We had no set itinerary; we would go where the weekend took us. With nothing but my toiletries, a revealing tank top, and some sparkly shoes in my bag, I stood in line amongst other fresh, energized twenty- and thirty-somethings with coffees in hand and travel playlists curated for the excitement we all felt. We weren't your typical commercial bus passengers. We were well-groomed and well-dressed, ready to hit the city the second we arrived. I handed my paper ticket to the driver with a smile as I boarded my chariot.

Ainsley and I had been friends since we met at grad school orientation. We had been through our highs and lows together, but as in grad school, we mostly spent our time dancing, drinking, and hooking up with guys. It's how we solved our problems. Or, more accurately, created then overcame our problems. She now lived in Tallahassee, where she had moved for a job a few years earlier but was seeking an escape from her life there. Specifically, from a fling-turned-relationship with a subordinate that had ended poorly. My low-cut tank and I were determined to cheer her up the best way I knew how.

This trip was also a great excuse to catch up with Angela, who had moved back to New York, where she had grown up, after completing her MBA at Georgetown. She had graciously offered to let us stay in her Midtown apartment, where Ainsley and I were planning to meet her later that afternoon.

In the meantime, Ainsley and I met up for lunch at a lovely understated Italian restaurant in Little Italy. We had been in the city for three hours, and our first bottle of wine sat empty on our outdoor table. Across the narrow, tourist-filled street from us was a much gaudier stereotypical Italian restaurant complete with red and white checkered tablecloths and wine bottle–candle holders. We had decided not to drink there because it was a little too family-friendly for our day-drinking intentions.

Ainsley perused the wine list as I read her a text from a guy I had started talking to online.

You're cute and I can't wait to meet you this Thursday. I'll probably try to kiss you. Be warned. It'll knock you off your feet, but then you're stuck. That's how it works. I'll come up with something good for us to do.

"Wow, he sounds cocky." She raised her eyebrow at me as I read the text. She then flagged down our waiter and ordered a second bottle of wine.

"Yeah, he is. I kinda like it."

When I began dating again after my depression it

seemed the whole landscape had changed. Free apps like OkCupid and Plenty of Fish had replaced the paid services like Match as the primary means of meeting people. Hooking up with a stranger at a bar was still a viable option, but my progressive recovery from binge eating had also healed the part of me that craved attention for the sake of attention. I still slept around from time to time, but the men I took home with me were men I was genuinely attracted to and wanted to get to know better. At least, for the night.

I had been testing out the online dating waters over the last few years, but I was already sick and tired of guys who hemmed and hawed over the most basic decisions. *Where should we go? I don't know. I like everything. I'm free whenever. What time's good for you?* I was in desperate need of a guy who could make a goddamn decision and take action. So far this guy I'd been chatting with seemed confident and capable.

"Besides," I continued as our waiter returned with a bottle of chilled Pinot Gris and poured out a small taste for Ainsley, "he was celebrating his birthday and was wasted when he sent that, and he still managed a coherent, grammatically correct message. He gets props for that. I'm actually excited about this one."

We killed the second bottle of wine over the next hour as we caught up with one another and then cabbed uptown to Angela's apartment, where we would be spending the night.

We shared emphatic greetings, and Angela took us on the grand tour of her one-bedroom apartment. We then quickly got ready for dinner and walked the six blocks, arriving just in time for our reservation. Seated at a small outdoor table at a crowded Mexican restaurant, we ordered our frozen margaritas and began to plan the rest of the evening. It was a warm summer night, and the combination of wine and margaritas had put us in the karaoke mood. Fortunately, New York had a million karaoke spots, including one right around the corner from the restaurant. We leisurely finished our gigantic beverages and even larger meals, then headed out on full stomachs, excited to blow off some steam.

A few short minutes later, we entered our private karaoke room and immediately placed orders for three rum and cokes (a drink Angela had ordered so much in our grad school days that we simply called it an "Angela"). We promptly programmed in as many terrible songs as the hour would allow. As we belted out the words to "Let's Hear it for the Boy," I felt a sense of calm take over me. Just as it did to Ainsley, this trip offered a much-needed escape from my own life. I didn't have to think or plan or tiptoe around the permanent fixture who lived on my couch back home. All I needed to do was drink and enjoy myself. And boy, did I.

After a little *NSYNC, a rousing rendition of "Don't Stop Believin'," and some hard-hitting Tiffany, we decided it was time to move on. Our next stop was a local bar, where we took a break from the hard alcohol and switched to beer. It was still early, and the bar was quiet enough for the three of us to chat and catch up about our jobs and our lack of love lives. Ainsley, now an epidemiologist, was extremely proficient at her job. In the years that I had been bungling around, bouncing from one entry-level position to the next, she had risen through the ranks and was managing several people. Angela worked in marketing for an online catalogue conglomerate. She enjoyed her work, but there was no room for growth and she, too, was looking for new employment. I was plotting to get them both to move back to DC. Or to a better city where I could eventually join them.

The crowd was just starting to pick up as "This Is How We Do It" blasted over the speakers. By reflex, I hopped off my stool and began to dance with the only other person at the bar who seemed as into Montell Jordan as I was. Rocco was well over six feet tall. He had a gold chain and a friendly smile. After the two of us finished rapping to the end of the song, he bought me a drink and escorted me back to my friends. There he regaled us with fascinating stories of his time working as a prison guard at Rikers Island, the maximum-security prison they always talked about on *Law & Order*. Rocco had seen it all, and we hung on his every word. He had been cussed out, spit on, and, on occasion, hit by inmates. One disgruntled felon, angered by a surprise inspection, had flung his own feces at Rocco, mostly missing him. *Mostly.*

We were closing in on midnight when Rocco took his leave. After surveying our surroundings and finding them or, rather, the crowd to be underwhelming, we decided it was time for a change in scenery. Angela mentioned a rooftop bar right across the street from her apartment. It was still a balmy eighty degrees out, and we loved the idea of continuing our drinking outside and being close to home when we needed to pass out.

We somehow made it several blocks and three flights of stairs to the gorgeous bar overlooking Midtown. After enjoying the view and ordering a round of drinks, we plopped down on a cushioned bench.

"Hey, are you with the birthday boy?" a good-looking guy in a plaid button-down to my right asked us.

I looked around. The bench we were sitting at was full of people doing shots, and one muscly guy wearing a pin that read, "It's my birthday!" We had unintentionally crashed a party.

"Yeah, we're with him." I pointed toward the birthday boy. Mr. Muscles looked our way and nodded.

"Looks like you girls need shots," he said with a laugh. His friend promptly flagged down the waitress and ordered three birthday cake shots for us. When they arrived, he and the friend who had ordered the shots moved down the bench to sit across from us, and we toasted the birthday boy. Familiar with how nights out with Ainsley and I went, and, sensing that we were going to be there for a while, Angela excused herself from the group to return home and get a decent night's sleep. She had plans the next morning and wasn't particularly interested in any of the guys at the party.

Ainsley and I loudly yelled our goodbyes and promised Angela we'd be quiet when we returned in a few hours. Fortunately for everyone, Ainsley had Angela's spare keys, so we could come and go as we pleased.

"What's your name?" I asked my new friend after Angela's departure.

"James," he slurred.

From that point on, things got kind of blurry. The hours of drinking seemed to have finally caught up with me, and before I knew it, Birthday James and I were up against the bar, making out frantically. He kept trying to lift up my shirt, and in my attempts to remain clothed, I accidentally knocked over a small table. Shortly after, a manager came over, politely interrupted with a gentle tap on my shoulder, and asked us to leave. Surveying the length of the now nearly empty bar, I noticed two bartenders wiping up spills and counting their tips. A single patron remained, casually sipping his beer, and the high-top tables were all vacant. Fortunately, that meant few people had seen, or noticed, our public groping session.

I spotted Ainsley on a bench along the wall by the stairs. She was making out with James's friend in a much less frenzied manner. I interrupted and informed Ainsley we'd been asked to leave. Her make-out buddy caught my friend's eye and headed over to the bar to settle the tab. As he left, Ainsley pulled me aside. "What do you want to do?" she asked. We were in New York, a city both of us had visited but neither of us really knew. I considered my options and decided I wanted to go home with James. Unlike previous nights I had shared with Ainsley during grad school, however, I felt in control of my decision. I was going to go home with James, not out of fear of being mundane or forgotten, but out of desire to have sex with an attractive guy while on vacation.

The boys returned and asked the inevitable question: Are you going to come home with us? Turns out, the guys were roommates. Jackpot! As long as Ainsley and I could stay in the same vicinity, we felt safe, and before we were able to say "yes," the guys had flagged down a cab and were giving the driver their address.

To our surprise, these guys worked on and lived near Wall Street. Their building was beautiful and the view from their ninth floor apartment, stunning. We exchanged a few words before splitting off and heading to the guys' respective bedrooms. Unfortunately for me, Birthday James had had far too much to drink that night and try as we might—and believe me, we tried!—sex wasn't in the cards. In the brief moments of consciousness before we both passed out, I noticed small, circular burns across James's otherwise flawless upper body. Cigarette burns, he told me bluntly when I asked. I could sense he didn't want to explain further, so I resumed kissing him until my head became too heavy to hold up.

I came to around 8 a.m., my head throbbing. James was still passed out next to me, face down on his sheets. I felt a lump under my back and attempted to shift positions, but my legs proved too stiff. I reached beneath me and discovered that I had passed out on his TV remote. That was going to be painful later.

I lay motionless as long as possible, silently begging the room to stop spinning. But my insatiable thirst finally proved enough to propel my aching body out of bed, through the living room, and into the bathroom. I was naked, but putting clothes on seemed too complicated in the moment. I stuck my face under the sink faucet and gulped cold water till it was spilling down my chest.

After a quick reprieve on the cool bathroom tile, I dragged myself back to the living room and decided to take a quick peek into the other bedroom to assess Ainsley's status. The door was ajar, so I pushed it open slightly. There, sleeping on top of the sheets, was my very naked friend and her very naked paramour. I clumsily retreated back to the living room, trying to erase that image forever from my brain, and returned to James's bedroom. James was awake and he seemed angry.

"Everything ok?" I inquired.

He was holding his phone. "Shit" was all he could say. "Shit. Shit. Shit."

I didn't have the energy to prod him, so I flung myself back into bed and waited for further explanation. Or sleep.

After a minute, or possibly much longer, he began to rant. "My brother was supposed to stay with me last night. He came all the way in from Jersey for my party. I don't remember if we told him we were leaving. He left me a bunch of messages, but I didn't hear my phone. Now he's not picking up. I don't know where he is. Fuck! He could be anywhere. Fuck!"

I tried my hardest to empathize with him, but given the way they were throwing money around the previous night, I couldn't imagine his brother wandering the streets all night looking for a warm grate to sleep on. He probably got himself a hotel room. Or went home with someone else—a girl or another friend. Or he might have just cabbed back to Jersey. But, the way James saw it, his brother was probably bleeding to death on a street corner somewhere in the city, and it was all my fault. I had distracted him with my sexuality. It happens.

I encouraged him to keep dialing his brother as I slowly and painfully dressed and slinked out to the living room to wait for Ainsley to emerge from the neighboring bedroom. I could feel the blood pulsing through my head with every heartbeat and was acutely aware of the terrible taste in my mouth. The night had been a fun little fantasy, but reality was proving to be a bitch. James was no longer the hot stranger I couldn't wait to go home with. He was a real person, with both real and imagined problems. I had no interest in staying and finding out more about him. When was Ainsley going to wake up?

While I waited, I checked my phone. Angela had texted me several times.

Where are you guys?

Are you ok?

Seriously, where are you?

Text me back as soon as you get this.

I felt terrible. Angela was a worrier by nature. Our disappearance could easily escalate into a police manhunt. I responded immediately, telling her that we were ok and heading back shortly. Then I texted Kat. *Ainsley and I drank ALL the booze in NY. I'm pretty sure I'm dying. Oh, and to get over softball James I slept with a Wall Street guy named James. Looks like I can close the chapter on that.* Then I stared at the wall until my eyes crossed.

A half hour later, the door to the second bedroom flung open and Ainsley and her fella appeared, both looking content. "How are you feeling?" Ainsley asked, surveying my disheveled appearance.

"Pretty much like I wanna die. And eat a whole bunch of fried food," I replied.

"Is that part of the weightlifting diet?" her bedfellow queried.

"Umm, what?" I had no idea what he was talking about.

"Are you allowed to eat fried foods when you're in training?" I was lost.

"Seriously, what?? Do you think I'm a weightlifter or something?"

"I mean... yeah. You told me you were. Last night. You were very specific. You told me all about your training schedule. Plus, you kind of look like you could be."

Ainsley burst out laughing. My head ached. "A

weightlifter?!" I racked my brain trying to remember the previous night. I had no recollection of even talking to this guy, let alone convincing him that I was a weightlifter. But it did sound like something I'd do. I liked messing with strangers when I was drinking.

Ainsley and her guy, Marco, sat down on the couch to my left, and the three of us settled into friendly conversation. He was pretty funny, and I briefly forgot that my body was shutting down. Unfortunately, James, hearing the laughter in the living room, decided to join us and ruin the fun. He recounted the story of his missing brother, adding that the brother had been located back in New Jersey, safe and sound. But the brother ended up spending a fortune on the limo ride home, and James was feeling guilty as hell. I didn't dare interrupt and point out that in a city with tens of thousands of cabs, taking a limo was the most expensive, most idiotic way to get home.

James then pulled out a bong and proceeded to take a hit. I looked at the clock. 9:00 a.m. Things were taking a turn for the worse, and Ainsley and I had places to be. As we got up to leave, Marco grabbed Ainsley's hand and told her she couldn't leave without checking out the view from the roof. James grumbled. He was as ready to be rid of me as I was of him. But he obligingly got up, and the four of us took the elevator to the roof. The view was stunning, after we adjusted our eyes to the glaring sunlight. We had a 360-degree panoramic view of the entire city. Ainsley and Marco began to kiss as James and I slowly distanced ourselves from each other.

"Ok, time to go. I'm starving," I said, interrupting the lovebirds.

"Geez, don't be such a weightlifter," Marco joked. The

three of us laughed, making James visibly angry.

We rode the elevator down to the guys' floor, where Ainsley kissed her companion goodbye. James and I barely made eye contact as he rushed off. Within minutes, Ainsley and I were in a cab heading back to Angela's. I rolled down the window to suck in the fresh air. It was another beautiful day, but I felt like hell.

Angela was gone when we arrived at her place. We walked in to find a box of donuts on the counter next to a note. "Thought you guys might be hungry." I couldn't remember the last time I was that happy. Ainsley hopped in the shower while I stuffed my face.

Fifteen minutes later, while slumped on the floor in front of Angela's couch, I heard a plea from the bathroom. "Jana, can you help me?" The water in the shower was still running. I dragged my crippled, but sated, body to the bathroom door and poked my head in. Ainsley was still in the shower. "I can't figure out how to turn it off." She sounded genuinely upset. "Can you do it?" I pulled back the shower curtain and stared blankly at the ancient plumbing. We were both far too hungover to complete basic tasks like showering. But after a few minutes of fiddling with an unnecessary number of knobs, the water was off and I returned to my spot on the floor, exhausted from my adventure.

I'm not entirely sure how we did it, but we managed to dress ourselves and muster enough energy to leave Angela's apartment. We spent the rest of the day eating and drinking with a friend of Ainsley's in SoHo. I stuck with water, but Ainsley got right back on the horse and was on her third beer when I left for the bus station. My headache had started to subside thanks to a handful of aspirin, but the nausea was taking hold. I missed the days in my mid-twenties when I could go out hard and wake up feeling fine the next day.

As I boarded my bus, I surveyed my companions: men and women in their twenties and thirties, heads down, faces half-obscured behind large sunglasses. Most were dressed in yoga pants or pajama bottoms, with bottles of Gatorade peeking out from their bags. I felt right at home. Though I looked and smelled like death, I had enjoyed a fun weekend with friends, gallivanted around New York, and spent the night with a hot, if volatile, stranger without feeling demeaned or insecure. I considered the weekend a win. And from the looks of it, I was surrounded by winners. At least, I pretended that was victory I smelled.

HOW TO LOSE
A GUY IN THREE WEEKS

I have an idea that you can feel free to veto. Watch the absolute worst movie of all time with me in Ballston this Thursday? It was a few days after my return from New York when I received the text from the cocky guy I had been chatting with online.

If you're talking 'Santa Versus the Martians' I'm in. But only if there's a guy and his two wise-cracking robots sitting front and center. I immediately regretted my obscure reference to *Mystery Science Theater 3000*, a show I assumed no one but my dad and I knew. I internally chastised myself, *I'm going to feel like an idiot when I have to explain that one to him.*

Less than a minute later he responded. *Do you know Mystery Science Theater?!* I inferred excitement from his text. Maybe I hadn't blown it.

Um, yeah. The show that was on in the 90s? Of course I know it, I added coolly, as I Googled, "Is MST3K still a thing?"

That's awesome! His text again screamed with enthusiasm. *Well, the guys who did the show do occasional live riffs that are broadcast in theaters nationwide. This Thursday they're riffing 'Manos Hands of Fate.' It's one of the worst movies of all time. Are you interested in going with me?*

An absolutely terrible movie with three grown men riffing over it the whole time... That sounded like possibly the best first date in the history of first dates. Granted, I had a very low standard for comparison. I allowed my texts to convey my excitement, and we made plans for later that week.

Do you want to meet at my place and I can drive us over, or do you prefer to Metro, in case I'm a serial killer?

Good question. I'll meet you at your place and you can drive. Just promise that if you're a serial killer you'll wait until after the movie to kill me.

I promise.

I briefly wondered if I should be so trusting of a total stranger. But I realized that after the movie I didn't really have anything big to look forward to until Thanksgiving. So killing me wouldn't really interfere with any exciting plans. I shrugged it off and turned on Bravo for another night of riveting reality TV.

I was more nervous than I could remember being on a first date as I exited the Metro and began walking toward his building, per the directions he had texted. I navigated the walking path that bisected a large group of apartment buildings, all of which appeared to have been built in '70s-style architecture with matching blue balconies.

I had become a pro at first dates in recent months. I no longer got nervous because I had come to understand that they generally didn't lead anywhere. In fact, I could be exceptionally charming when faced with a guy I had no interest in, which was, unfortunately, most of the time. Yet, as I continued my walk, scanning each passerby far too intensely for their own comfort, I was unnerved by the sweatiness of my palms.

Finally, I saw a bald head moving toward me along the path. This must be him, I thought as I dried my hands one more time on my pants. We made eye contact, smiled, and shared the awkward hug of two people who have chatted for some time but have never actually met. *Damn*, I thought, *no attraction. I hope the movie's good.*

My confidence returned as my lack of attraction to JD sunk in, and we chatted spiritedly as he drove us to the Ballston Commons Mall in Arlington, Virginia. Conversation was easy, and he was certainly as funny as his online interactions had led me to believe he'd be. Most people are afraid to discuss the Holocaust on a first date, but not JD. He wondered aloud if Anne Frank's diary would have carried as much weight if it had been written in a Lisa Frank neon-unicorn journal. We both suspected it wouldn't.

We had such a great time chatting over dinner before the show that we arrived late to the theater. Surprised to see a full house for such an odd movie choice, we parked ourselves in the very front row, craned our necks upward, and joined in with the rest of the audience, already convulsing with laughter. The show did not disappoint. For two solid hours I laughed—not a coy, adorable first-date laugh, but loud guffawing that actually made me vibrate in my seat and made my nose run a little. Thankfully, JD was staring at the screen and not at me, because that kind of laughing does not get a girl a second date. And, by the time he reached over to hold my hand (not the one I had been using to wipe my nose), I knew I wanted a second date. The physical attraction may have been lacking, but I had to admit there was chemistry. That, or I was dizzy from laughing. Either way, I felt great.

The ride home was uneventful, but nice. Conversation continued to flow easily and he did not, in fact, try to kill me. As he pulled up outside of my building, I remembered his initial text the night of his birthday, before my whirlwind trip to New York: *I'll probably try to kiss you. Be warned. It'll knock you off your feet, but then you're stuck. That's how it works.*

I decided to linger and wait for the kiss. It more than lived up to the hype. And, it was the first time in a long time I didn't need to wipe off the area around my mouth afterward. *Damn*, I thought as he drove away, *that was kind of perfect.*

Three days later, I prepared for our second date: dinner and a movie at his place. I rarely made it to second dates these days, usually because of lack of interest on my part, but I knew enough from watching people on TV to know that dinner and a movie at someone's apartment was code for hooking up. I didn't know where exactly the night was going to lead, but I was excited to be going out with a guy with whom I enjoyed spending time. I brushed my teeth, spritzed on my only perfume (a free sample from Sephora), and switched from my comfortable weekend full-coverage cotton underwear into purple lacy underwear that was cute, but not presumptuous. I didn't want my underwear to make the wrong statement, should they make an appearance. I rummaged through my drawers to find the cutest bra I had (that didn't have underwire poking out through a hole or errant strands dangling off from too many washes). Unlike the women on TV, I did not have matching bra and underwear sets for every day of the week in case of impromptu intercourse. If a guy on the Metro caught my eye and whisked me off to his apartment on a regular old Tuesday, he'd be less than thrilled when he stripped me down to my faded polka dot briefs and beige full-coverage bra with wide straps for extra support.

I did the best with what I had, and, dressed in my Target finery, I Metroed to JD's place, switching the bottle of wine I was carrying back and forth between my sweaty hands. His spacious one-bedroom apartment smelled of apple pie–scented candles, and he smelled even better.

I awkwardly opened the bottle of wine and began wandering around his apartment as he tended to the steaks he was searing. It had been years since a guy had cooked a meal for me, and I ate it up, literally and figuratively. Everything was delicious, and, though I still wasn't altogether physically attracted to him, I hung on his every word.

After dinner, we moved to the couch. The guys who created and voiced *Mystery Science Theater 3000* also had a website, Rifftrax.com, where you could download or purchase videos synced with their hilarious commentary. JD had downloaded *Plan 9 from Outer Space*, a movie not generally lauded for its romantic undertones. As I sipped my wine in between laughs, he put his arm around me.

After the movie ended, we watched a few short clips from the Rifftrax website, including a ten-minute piece explaining how women could maximize their efficiency at the grocery store. It was the oddest seduction I'd ever been a part of, but it worked. Before I even knew it was happening, JD had placed my wine glass on the coffee table, and we were clawing at each other as if I had just saved ten dollars at the market.

I hadn't intended to have sex with him. In fact, on the Metro ride over, I thought about ways to defer sex until the third or fourth date, as I assumed a lady should. I was still feeling out my dating strategy. I wasn't really sure how long I was supposed to wait, but TV had led me to believe it was important to wait, to make him work for it if the guy actually had potential to be a boyfriend and not just a hookup. But when JD took my hand and led me to his bedroom, I didn't resist. He took charge, and I was along for the ride. And what a fantastic ride it was.

After the first round, we curled up together in bed, and, after a few moments of silence, he asked me an unusual question: what was I most scared of? After my initial reaction of, *OMG, this is exactly the type of thing that happens in romantic comedies*—they have sex and talk all night and it's sweet and funny and perfect... I realized that my answer was in no way Julia Roberts-esque and probably wouldn't lead to some amazing revelation like that we were both afraid of falling in love too fast.

"Ghosts," I answered.

"Ghosts?"

"Yeah, ghosts. I'm pretty sure my parents' house in Connecticut is haunted. I know it's not a poltergeist because my parents built the house, and they had to blast through solid slate to set the foundation. So, no Native American burial ground. But there's something in that house and it creeps me out."

And as often happens when I discuss the creepy things

that happened in my house in Connecticut—strange voices, bloody footprints appearing out of nowhere, appliances turning on and off in the middle of the night— I strayed into other, lesser (but no less arbitrary) fears. Having watched *The Twilight Zone* at much too early an age growing up, I also harbored a deep-seated fear of Baby Dimples, the antique doll that had been passed down from my grandmother to my mother and then to me. It wore a baptismal gown, blinked when its head moved, and had lived in my bedroom in Connecticut. I was pretty sure it planned to kill me someday.

As I divulged the details of my ridiculous fears, I tried to visualize Julia Roberts or Meg Ryan lying in the arms of a handsome Hugh Grant or Tom Hanks-like suitor, talking about their fear of ghosts and demonic dolls. I couldn't. Their writers were far too savvy for that.

Thankfully, JD's answer, once I finally stopped rambling about the supernatural, was almost as stupid.

"Bees?" I questioned.

Granted, his reasons for fearing bees were much more reality-based than my fears—he was allergic. But still, bees?

JD didn't have much else to say after that; he was ready for round two and so was I. Somehow my rambling hadn't completely turned him off, and I wasn't going to ruin any more potential movie moments by talking.

I awoke the next morning in his sun-filled room. We were lying next to each other naked, but the romance from the previous night's *Plan 9* viewing and late-night discussion of all things terrifying was gone. I suddenly regretted jumping so quickly into bed with a guy I still wasn't entirely attracted to. He was completely pale from head to toe, and, despite the fact that it was the end of summer, he didn't even have the hint of a tan line. He was ghostly, which, as we had established the previous night, was terrifying to me. And in addition to having no hair on the top of his head, his eyebrows were so light that it looked like he didn't have any at all. He had a great body though, and he clearly knew how to use it. Still, part of me was wishing I had awoken in bed next to softball James. I quickly admonished myself for lying in bed with one guy and fantasizing about another. Who knew when I'd be having sex again? I should just enjoy it. With that, I turned to face JD. He pulled me into his arms, and I forgot all about James.

I planned the third date. In an attempt to get out of the dinner-and-a-movie rut, I suggested we head out to the Dogfish Head Alehouse in Maryland for their Oktoberfest release party. The website touted it as a night of beer, games, and live music.

The night started out benignly enough. While we were waiting for a table in the restaurant, we grabbed some Oktoberfest and chatted while groups of partygoers played cornhole and ladder ball. Poorly.

JD discussed his aspiration to win some unpopular Olympic sport so that he could get his picture on a cereal box. I talked about my interest in parasites and other neglected tropical diseases. My grad degree was in emerging infectious diseases, and as part of my degree requirements I had spent a couple weeks in Panama tracking the spread of the highly infectious and occasionally deadly hantavirus. JD and I held hands while I painted sexy images in his mind of me in a portable HEPA air purifying helmet, sweaty from a day setting traps in the Panamanian forest, collecting blood samples from the eyes of the mice we caught. I sure knew how to woo a man.

We ate in the air-conditioned dining room of the brewery, then returned outside to grab more Oktoberfest and listen to a blues band that had just taken the stage. By now, JD had stopped drinking, since he was driving us home. He informed me that he had taken some blues dancing lessons a while back and wanted to dance. He then grabbed my hand and led me to the vacant dance floor, where he spun and dipped me, dancing me around in front of groups of drunken onlookers. I couldn't stop smiling.

Just a few songs in, the band took a break. JD and I were sweaty and disheveled and apparently completely turned on. Holding my hand, he walked me back to the car. As I went to open the door, he pressed me up against it and kissed me. I was powerless to stop it. I probably would have had sex with him right there in the parking lot if the owner of the car next to us hadn't shown up. I smiled at the couple opening the doors to their SUV as I took my hands out from under JD's shirt.

My hand remained firmly planted on his upper thigh the entire ride home. At every red light, we made out like teenagers who couldn't have sex at home because their parents were waiting up for them. He pulled into his parking lot, and before he even had his seatbelt off, I was unzipping his pants. I couldn't for the life of me remember ever being that turned on before. It was then, while I was going down on him in the front seat of his car, that I had a crystallizing moment—I finally understood women who said they enjoyed giving head. I kind of always assumed they were lying, trying to make themselves sound better than the rest of us. Don't get me wrong, I wasn't against going down on a guy. It was the polite thing to do if I eventually wanted him to reciprocate. But still, I had never truly enjoyed it before, perhaps because I had never been involved with a guy I really liked.

As I bobbed up and down, pondering the sad state of my cumulative love life, JD clenched. "Security," he managed to moan. I sat up and saw a white vehicle with yellow blinking lights slowly drive by. The job wasn't yet complete, but I felt satisfied that I had enjoyed myself so much doing something I generally ranked on par with vacuuming.

Though temporarily interrupted, our lust persisted. Holding hands, we raced up to his apartment and barely managed to close the door behind us. I don't remember taking the time to disrobe, but as I took my position on my knees in his entryway I was aware of our clothes strewn around me. Unfortunately, the Oktoberfest seemed to be hitting me hard, and, though kneeling, I began to sway. I steadied myself against JD's thighs to keep from tilting into the wall. JD could tell things were not going to proceed in his favor if we stayed where we were, so he guided me to his bed, which proved to be a much easier surface to work on.

The next morning, I had plans to meet a visiting friend downtown, but the sound of JD's alarm was extremely unwelcome. Still, as consciousness took hold and I saw JD lying next to me, it suddenly hit me just how attracted to him I was. I was finally hooked.

I got dressed and we kissed goodbye. I wasn't going to see him for a whole week, as we both had plans to go out of town for Labor Day at the end of the coming week. The realization that I was going to miss him made me happy.

I had plans that morning with a friend from college, Nadine. During our sophomore year she had suggested, during a particularly dangerous game of Here's-What-Bothers-Me-Most-About-You, that maybe I was dead inside. She was concerned that I exhibited no range of emotions. I was always placid, always had a smile plastered on my face. Given the way I was starting to feel about JD, it was nice to finally get confirmation that I probably wasn't a sociopath. I was just a stereotypical middle child who had spent her life playing peacekeeper, negotiating other people's feelings at the expense of her own in order to avoid conflict. At the time it had struck me as odd that anyone would even care how I felt, as long as we all got along.

It had been several years since I'd last seen Nadine. As I rode the Metro downtown to the hotel where she and her family were staying, I brimmed with excitement. I was excited about how things were going with JD! I was excited to see Nadine! I was excited to tell Nadine I had actual human emotions!

She and her husband had come down from New York that weekend for a wedding with their two young children in tow. Though they had only been in the hotel for two nights, every inch of the room was covered in clothes, toys, or electronics. When I walked in, Nadine was nursing her five-month-old son, Asher, while her three-year-old, Eli, vied for attention by dancing and singing in front of her. I dodged tiny swinging arms and stepped around toy trucks and Dr. Seuss books to give Nadine a hug hello.

They had been awake since 6 a.m., when Asher woke up screaming, and had already all had one breakfast that morning. The plan was to go someplace quick nearby to catch up before they headed back to New York. Ten o'clock came and went as Asher spit up on the only two clean outfits he had left. While my friend stripped him for the third time, the rest of us went into crisis mode, as Eli couldn't find his precious toy airplane. On hands and knees, we scoured the hotel room looking for said airplane. By 10:30 a.m., the plane had been located and Asher was wearing a previous outfit that had been deemed "clean enough."

By 11 a.m., we were all seated around a small table at Le Pain Quotidien, a cafe chain in the District. I watched my friend cut up Eli's meal into child-friendly pieces and encourage him to eat his fruit. It was hard to reconcile the person before me with the girl I had known in college. She and I had made out at a bar one New Year's Eve. She got me my first vibrator. She had instructed me, step-by-step, on how to give a proper blow job. She couldn't wait to tell me all about her first really great orgasm, and I couldn't wait to hear. Now, sitting with her family, she seemed so mature and "adult." I was still gossiping with friends about vibrators and orgasms.

Just before I got to pitying myself for not having a career or a husband or children, she asked me what I had done the previous night. With her husband firmly engaging Eli in a discussion about colors, I leaned in and said, "I drank, danced, and had sex with a really hot guy." Without skipping a beat, she sighed and said, "God, I'm so jealous. Can we trade lives?" It was the first time anyone had ever been jealous of me. For anything. Ever. It felt fantastic.

I was still working hard to meet new people, since everyone I worked with was over forty and had a family, and my roommate, Mr. Antisocial, made it so that I never wanted to be home. So, two days later, when a girl from my NIH softball team asked me to join her and her friends for happy hour, I jumped at the opportunity.

Over half-priced drinks, we chatted about our lives and how we all knew one another. Most of the girls were single, which made me extremely happy given that the majority of my friends were in serious relationships or married and tended not to want to go clubbing or indulge in lengthy conversations about the misadventures of dating. This group of girls seemed more amenable to my idea of a fun night out. One of the girls then asked me if I was seeing anyone. I laughed, as is my normal reaction to the question. "God no," I responded by rote. Then I caught myself. "Hmm, well, maybe. I'm not sure. I've gone out on three dates with this one guy…" The girls were immediately interested. I had their rapt attention, so of course, instead of downplaying the dates, I gushed about a boy I liked to a group of women I had never met before. By the end, they were telling me exactly what I wanted to hear based on the version of events that I had crafted with my selective memory—that it sounded like JD really liked me, that guys don't act like that with girls they're only sort-of interested in. I left the bar feeling great about my relationship with JD.

As if sensing my self-satisfaction mixed with a slight edge of tipsiness, JD texted me seconds after I parted ways with the girls. The text read in part: *Random, I know, but how would you feel about wiping out a plague with me this evening?*

After a moment of confusion, I remembered our (lengthy) discussion about parasites and diseases at the Oktoberfest party. I also was vaguely aware of seeing a board game called Pandemic on one of his shelves while pinned against his wall. He was asking me over to play a board game about diseases! A girl can't really ask for much more. I hopped on the train and met him at his place.

JD prepared dinner and poured us both wine, then proceeded to explain the game to me. I was a little preoccupied by having just been told by complete strangers how much this guy they'd never met must really like me, but I picked up enough of what he was saying to start playing. I gave him some shit after a first wave of disease hit Algiers, but he just smiled and said, "So this is what I get for wanting to see you one more time before I leave for Atlanta?" Though we inevitably doomed humanity to death by pandemic, I considered the night a success.

Flying high on wine and disease-talk, JD and I made out for a bit on his couch as pieces of clothing were slowly removed. Having only just discovered how great giving blow jobs could be, I got down on my knees and thanked JD properly for a great night.

Several days later, my plane touched down in Nashville, and Ainsley and Angela greeted me at the gate with a cold beer in hand. Since we now lived in different states, we had begun a tradition of meeting each year in a new city and enjoying a long weekend of fun. This year was Nashville. The previous two years had taken us to

New Orleans and Austin.

After dumping our luggage in our room, we headed to the hotel bar to start the trip off right—with tequila shots. Within minutes of shooting our drinks, we were approached by a group of men, all middle-aged, covered with Gamecocks paraphernalia. Turns out they had traveled to Nashville for the South Carolina–Vandy game earlier that evening. Though Carolina had lost, the men were in good spirits and made for some great company. Two younger guys eventually joined the group, and we all chatted jovially as we drank. I realized that my usual instinct would have been to flirt, and potentially sleep with one of the younger guys, yet even after my third tequila shot I felt nothing. Apparently, I had learned from JD how much better sex could be if you knew and enjoyed your companion. Still, I was a little jealous as I watched Ainsley leave with the most attractive guy in the group.

That jealousy remained the next morning. After Ainsley had made her way back to our room (aided by the room number I had written on her hand before she left the bar, just in case), we got the full story. She had had fantastic hotel stranger sex. Unfortunately, it turned out, the guy had a kid and was staying at the hotel with the child's mother, who may or may not have also been his girlfriend. Ainsley was vague on the details. The guy did spring for a separate hotel room in which to have sex, but left Ainsley at 6 a.m. so he could sneak back into the room he was sharing with the (possible) girlfriend unnoticed.

As she described the night—the sex, the awkward exchange as the dude slinked out of the room at first light, her struggle to find our room in her still-drunk haze after, I was conflicted by how I felt. I knew I didn't need drunken hookups to have fun on vacation, especially hookups rife with unnecessary drama, but I still loved telling drunken hookup stories. And this one was a doozy.

The next night, after touring the Ryman Auditorium—an historic music venue where Elvis, Patsy Cline, and Johnny Cash had all performed—and the Country Music Hall of Fame, we stopped in Robert's Western World, a well-known country music bar featuring great bands, for a live music fix. The air smelled distinctly of bourbon, and I could almost taste the chicken wings being served up to the patrons at the packed bar. After a bit of awkward hovering, we were able to claim a table toward the back of the room and were ready for a show.

Immediately, I was taken by the band's upright bass player. This was unusual, as I generally wasn't attracted to musicians. In fact, hearing that a guy was in a band was a major turn-off for me, perhaps because I had dated a musician once. I'd had to attend his shows and feign interest in his music when, truthfully, it wasn't that good. And most guys on the online dating sites I frequented fancied themselves musicians, as if they assumed women everywhere were hot for guys who could strum a few chords or kill it on Expert Mode in Rock Band. "Musicians" were a dime a dozen, and I was too frugal to buy in.

This musician was different. He was slapping the upright bass, his fingers moving faster than I thought possible. Add to that, he was singing Leroy Van Dyke's "The Auctioneer," his mouth moving in time with his fingers. He was clearly talented. I desperately wanted to know what else his mouth and hands could do with such quick precision, and I made numerous obnoxious comments along those lines to my friends.

As luck would have it, the band took a break right about the time my libido had reached its peak, and they sent their bassist around with a jar to collect tips. With a dollar bill in hand, I pulled my shirt down slightly and waited for Mr. Bass Man. He approached our table and smiled the smile of someone who works for tips. I gave him my dollar and asked him how long he'd been with the band. He said something, but I didn't bother listening. I was already picturing him playing me like his bass.

While lost in my lusty fantasy, I was vaguely aware of him winking at me and walking off to collect from the next table.

"What is wrong with you?" Ainsley asked when he was clearly out of earshot. As my partner in crime, she knew what I was capable of when I set my mind to something. "You barely said two words to him. Go talk to him."

I turned and saw the bassist, Billy, receding into the crowd. I didn't move. "I think I'm broken," I announced after a quick internal assessment.

In the past, when faced with an attractive guy in a city I was likely never going to visit again, I would rise to the occasion and charm my way into his bed. Or at least share a very public moment of gratuitous groping before moving on to the next bar. Yet suddenly, the chase had lost its thrill.

"Is it because of that guy you're seeing?" Angela suggested.

"What? No!" I responded indignantly. "We've only gone on four dates. I'm free to sleep with anyone I want, and so is he." But even as I said it, I knew that he was the reason I was never going to know, personally, what Billy's hands could do. And the sudden thought that JD was in

Atlanta sleeping with other girls made me upset, both with him and with myself. I was not supposed to like someone so much after four dates that I'd walk away from a perfectly hot bass player and his profoundly muscular forearms.

The rest of the weekend played out much the same way. We were out till last call every night listening to great live music, surrounded by guys buying us drinks, and I didn't so much as try to take off anyone's pants. One guy did shout out, "Great tits!" and proceeded to shove his tongue down my throat. But even that was less satisfying than usual, and after allowing him a few seconds to feel me up, I extricated myself from his paws. JD had ruined my Nashville weekend, and I was acutely aware that he hadn't called or texted the entire trip.

Returning home, exhausted and storyless, I took solace in the fact that I'd likely be hearing from JD soon. But the end of the holiday weekend came and went with no word from him.

This is stupid, I eventually told myself. *I like this guy. I can text him and tell him I want to see him. I'm a strong, independent woman who just really wants to hang out with the boy she likes.*

Text sent. No response.

Hours went by. Hours I was painfully aware of because I checked my phone every five minutes. Finally, just as I was simultaneously convincing myself that I was better off without him and making very dramatic bargains with God concerning the future of my relationship with JD, I got a response. He was free Thursday! All was right with the world. I had freaked out for nothing. *He's clearly into me*, I thought, reminding myself of the sage words of the girls

I had happy houred with, two of whom I could no longer name. And with that, I got myself overly excited about Thursday.

I had suggested dinner halfway between our apartments since it was, after all, a work night. On the walk there, I felt a brief moment of uneasiness. We had barely spoken since our romantic Pandemic board game night over a week ago. *What if he dumps me over dinner?* On cue, my brain retrieved long dormant memories of the night, years ago, when I had broken up with Everett mid-dinner. It had been painful to be the dumper. I certainly didn't want to be the dumpee.

I walked into P.F. Chang's distracted by memories of that horrible night. JD was already there waiting. As I walked up, he smiled at me, and with his hand on my lower back as the waiter guided us to our table, all of my anxiety disappeared. *I can't believe how crazy I let myself get*, I chided myself. *I don't hear from him for a few days, and I assume he's dumping me? I'm an idiot.*

I returned my attention to my date. We shared the Dinner for Two special and discussed our respective trips. I left out the part about the bass player. I wondered what he left out.

As we finished our desserts, red velvet cake and tiramisu, JD checked his watch. *Shit*, my crazy mind started racing. *He's got other places to be.* I prepared myself for what was coming.

"Do you want to go to Dave & Buster's?" It was right next door. "It's still early."

I vowed not to let my brain get in the way for the rest of the night.

Over the next hours we played a few games—Skee-

Ball, car racing, first-person shooters. "I assume you don't wanna go home just yet," he said as we walked toward the parking lot. He assumed correctly. It was only ten o'clock and I was in no mood to say goodnight.

Back at his place, he asked if I had ever seen the movie *Kung Pow!* I hadn't. He smiled at me and said, "I think you'll like it." I immediately knew I would.

The movie was hilarious and terrible, and I loved it. What I loved more was the way he rubbed my leg with the arm he had wrapped around me and the way he kissed the top of my head throughout the movie. I wasn't used to this kind of constant affection, and I took it as a sign that we'd be sharing many more nights together like this.

As so often happens after a funny movie (or disease-themed board game or walk to the car), I was ready to go. We stood, and I started walking to the bedroom. As I did so, he wrapped his arms around me from behind, pulled me tight against him, and began kissing the back of my neck. My knees began to buckle, and thankfully he spun me around and had me up against the wall, arms pinned over my head. The next few hours were a fantastic blur as we made our way from room to room, eventually finding our way to his bed. Afterward, he wrapped me in his arms and showed me pictures and videos from his trip.

I awoke early, but contented. JD walked me to his door but was too tired to walk me out. We kissed goodbye and I was on my merry way.

I spent the next few days telling any of my friends who would listen about JD. I asked advice about when it was appropriate to have the "relationship" talk. Most of my friends agreed that the talk should happen before sleeping with the guy. Oops.

A week later, it began to gnaw at me that I hadn't heard from JD. Since we were practically dating, I texted him Thursday to see if he was free that weekend to hang out. No response.

Remembering how I had freaked out the last time I didn't immediately hear back from him, I opted to give him the benefit of the doubt. *Maybe he's super busy and has to work late and his iPhone battery died*, I rationalized as I sipped some Three Olives Grape Vodka.

Getting drunk certainly helped time move quicker, but by midday Saturday, I still hadn't received a reply. With my three closest friends out of town that weekend, I was determined to find ways to keep myself busy.

A day at the zoo sounded like just the distraction I needed. But, as it turns out, a Saturday at the zoo is one of the worst places a lonely girl can go. Everyone at the zoo was paired off. There were older couples flaunting their families in my face, younger couples holding hands and laughing at inside jokes, and brand-new couples who all seemed to stop right next to me to make out with each other. Even the animals had mates because, as the signs indicated with few exceptions, they needed companionship to thrive. You know you have it bad when you're jealous of a lemur.

I stretched out my day with as much activity as I could think of, but ended up home alone that Saturday night. Panic was beginning to set in. After realizing I hadn't received a single call or text that day, I clung to one shining thread of hope. *Maybe my phone's broken!* I was giddy at the thought. I immediately texted Kat and told her it was urgent she respond if she got my message. She didn't know it, but my sanity was hanging in the balance.

For one blissful hour I heard nothing. *JD's probably been trying to get in touch with me this whole time*, I consoled myself. I was feeling quite foolish about my second overreaction, until I heard the distinctive chime of my phone signaling a new message. I stared down at it with hatred. *Why are you doing this to me?* I wanted to scream.

The message was from Kat. She had received my text.

As hard as I then tried to convince myself that maybe my phone was only sending and receiving select messages, picking and choosing who I was in contact with, I knew it was a losing battle. I settled into the tub with my bottle of grape vodka and spent the remainder of the weekend drinking the previous three weeks away.

It was a sad commentary on my life that the best consecutive three weeks in my recent memory hadn't mattered enough to JD for him to even manage a text telling me it was over. No generic *sorry, just not feelin it* ☹ message. No explanation. Much like the Eastern Hemisphere during our game of Pandemic, my relationship with JD was a lost cause.

A GHOST STORY

I believe in ghosts. Or, more accurately, I'm afraid of ghosts; I have been ever since I caught the tail end of *Poltergeist* on TV as a young child. Though for most of my life it had been a purely irrational fear.

And then, one night in 1997 while I was asleep, I heard a gentle knock on my bedroom door. "Jana, wake up. It's time for school," I heard my mother's voice say as the door opened. I had been woken from a dead sleep, so I was groggy and mumbled something to affirm that I was awake. I slowly dragged myself out of bed to the bathroom to brush my teeth and returned to my room to change. As I sat on the edge of my bed pulling my sneakers on, still half asleep, I looked at my clock. 4:30 a.m. Also, it very quickly dawned on me, it was July. I immediately returned to bed. The next afternoon, when I had gotten the full twelve hours of sleep required by my teenage body, I asked my mom why she had gotten me up for school in the middle of the night in July. She looked as confused as I suddenly felt and responded that she hadn't come into my room the previous night.

Several years earlier, I had started experiencing regular episodes of sleep paralysis—essentially when your mind wakes up before your body does and you're stuck in a REM-induced paralytic state while fully aware of your surroundings. Often, these episodes were accompanied by sensations of being suffocated by an unidentifiable creature compressing my chest—all the while I would be unable to scream or run away. I assumed the voice from the night before was loosely related to my terrifying sleep issues, so I shrugged it off and didn't think about it again. Until the following July.

"Jana, wake up. It's time for school." My mother's voice was once again preceded by a knock and followed by the sound of my bedroom door opening. I jolted awake, but remained on my side, facing the wall. I didn't want to see whatever or whoever had opened my door. Then, while fully clenched and wondering how to escape, I felt the edge of my mattress sink as someone sat on the bed next to me.

I freaked out, threw off my covers, and turned over, ready to run. But my room was dark and empty. My door was closed. It was 4:30 a.m.

Sufficiently terrified, I did my best to rationalize what had happened. Something must have triggered a memory of that weird night from a year ago, and I was just having a very realistic dream about it. I was still experiencing intermittent sleep paralysis, so conscious nightmares weren't entirely out of the realm of possibility.

And then, the following July: *Knock. Knock.* "Jana, wake up. It's time for school." My bedroom door opened, and I felt the intruder perch on the edge of my bed. I didn't move. My heart was racing, and I kept my eyes shut tight—until I felt pressure across my chest and arms, as if someone was leaning down to hug me while I slept. My eyes shot open and I bolted upright in bed as my body trembled and my terrified brain struggled to assess my surroundings. Nothing. The only thing my eyes could see in that moment before they adjusted to the dark was the red glow of my digital clock informing me it was 4:30.

Just over a year later, while home for the summer after completing my freshman year at BU, I was sitting around the dinner table with my family. My summer job interning in a biology lab at a local university made it impossible for me to sleep my desired twelve hours a night, and my sleep deprivation was noticeable in the way I responded to questions about my day with one-word answers or grunts of annoyance.

"You look tired." My mother's assessment was on point, but all I could do was nod in affirmation. "Are you going to be able to get up for work tomorrow? Should I check in and make sure you're up?"

My mother's kind offer to wake me up in the morning triggered my memory. I was suddenly aware it was August. I had made it through July without another visitation from the ghost. *Why?* I wondered. *What had changed?* Perhaps the ghost, irritated that I never actually got up and left for school at her urging, had given up on me. Perhaps she recognized that I had graduated and was effectively an adult, capable of taking care of myself (for the most part). Perhaps she had accepted a more interesting gig haunting an abandoned mental ward or a pet cemetery. Regardless of her reasons, she was gone.

And yet, despite such a mundane ending to the dullest ghost story ever told, I'm still afraid of ghosts. Not because I believe they'll do me harm, but because I don't know what they'll do. I thrive on predictability and rationality. Ghosts are disruptive by nature, unbound by logic, unpredictable.

The same can be said of men who ghost. They may not cause me physical harm, but they can make me question what I thought I knew, stir up sudden feelings of instability and insecurity in my otherwise orderly life. Sadly, while ghosts are rare and ephemeral, the men who ghost are everywhere, indistinguishable from everyone else, ready to wreak havoc on my life at any moment. And that is downright terrifying.

DEARLY DEPARTED

Bathroom selfie. *Nope.* Shirtless selfie. *Nope.* Shirtless bathroom selfie. *Definitely not.* I was two weeks back into the online dating tedium, scrolling through a mélange of similar and disappointing profiles, when I received a message from a guy named Eric. His messages were witty and extremely flattering. Somehow he was funny, hot, and into me. Yep, this had all the makings of major heartbreak. And, after perusing his pictures, then his profile, then his pictures again, I decided to dive right in. He was average height and on the slender side, but his dark brown hair and messy-on-purpose beard framed his smiling face perfectly and accentuated his blue eyes. Just a few short months after being ghosted by JD, it looked like things were finally going my way.

We messaged each other daily, our conversations becoming longer and funnier over time. His jokes were like poetry, sweeping me off my feet. At least, that's my understanding of what poetry's supposed to do to women. In all honesty, the only poem I ever liked was "The Raven." And from my recollection, Poe wasn't exactly a ladies' man...unless you're counting cousins.

After a week and a half of rushing home to read his messages on my computer—I didn't yet have a smartphone and apps weren't even a thing at the time—and working diligently to craft my own witty responses, I suggested it was time to meet. I was terrified when he accepted because I knew he was far too attractive for me. *Maybe, just maybe, I can win him over with my personality*, I thought. It had happened in movies plenty of times, though in those cases it was always portly, inept men winning over beautiful women with their accidental bravery and witty retorts. As far as I knew, there was no version of that story where a charming and funny, but otherwise ordinary woman, won over the Ryan Gosling character by hopping on a Segway and thwarting a mall robbery attempt.

No sooner had he accepted my invitation for drinks than the media outlets began chirping with news of a hurricane set to pummel the East Coast. An unexpected and underreported derecho, a storm system similar to a tornado, had crippled the DC metro area earlier that year, and the East Coast was not about to be caught underprepared. Around the time I was planning to go on a first date with Eric, the city was shutting down, literally. Metro service was suspended and all nonessential government employees and contractors like me were given two days off of work to hunker down and stay safe. I couldn't get anywhere, and we were told to brace for a possible week without power. I, of course, stocked up on the essentials: Skinnygirl sangria, vodka, toilet paper, peanut butter, and apples. Bring on the hurricane.

I spent my first hurricane day off baking, so as to use

up all of my perishable items before we lost power. As I piped ganache, crushed peppermint candies, melted chocolate over a double boiler, and licked batter off beaters, text messages poured in from Eric. The hurricane gave him a reprieve from his job as a paralegal, but he filled his hurricane-waiting hours studying for the law school classes he took at night. I read and reread every text with glee as we waited for the hurricane that would barely hit us.

Over the next few days, the texts kept coming—sweet, hilarious, making me deliriously giddy. By some miracle he seemed to think I was funny, and I spent hours crafting texts to continue the ruse. I didn't bother mentioning that I didn't have an unlimited texting plan with my old-school slider phone. He was worth the extra ten cents per text message. There weren't many guys I could say that about. I had, in fact, once ended things with a guy I was only moderately interested in because the texting had become too expensive.

Superstorm Sandy, as the hurricane came to be known, had spared the DC metro area, devastating much of the Jersey shore and Manhattan instead. Eric and I had yet to reschedule our first date, and I was losing patience. The next Sunday night, as I was settling in for my reality TV fix, I texted him, asking if we were ever going to meet. He immediately called me, explaining that he was in the Bethesda area, not far from my Rockville apartment, and would love to see me that night. Also, his phone was dying, so we had to act fast.

While I wanted to see him, I wasn't expecting him to suggest that night. Given the hour and my unkempt appearance I should have declined, postponing for a more appropriate day and hour, but I was so excited to finally meet him that I accepted without first thinking back to the last time I had washed my hair (Friday morning) or considering what time the Metro stopped running (12am). Eric didn't know the Rockville area well, so I threw out some places I knew in Rockville Town Center, just a few Metro stops north.

"Is there a Buffalo Wild Wings there?" he asked. I wasn't positive but responded that I thought there was.

"Great, we could try that!" He sounded excited. I began to sweat.

"Metro's single-tracking today, so it'll take me a little while to get there. Wanna meet in an hour?" No response. His phone had died. *Shit,* I thought. *Is he on his way there now? Did we actually make plans? Is he expecting me to go? Is there a Buffalo Wild Wings in Rockville?*

The more I thought about it, the more my anxiety grew. I was already in my pajamas, I had just washed my face, and my hair was knotted in a bun atop my head. I couldn't meet him looking the way I did. If I put on makeup, threw on a cute outfit, and attempted to wrangle my hair into a cute ponytail, I could probably look decent. But decent is not enough when you're about to meet someone you find insanely attractive for the first time.

In addition to the issues with my physical appearance, there was the Metro to consider. By the time I got to Rockville Town Center, it would practically be time to leave. If I was going to win Eric over with my personality, I was going to need time. And probably deodorant. I was screwed.

If his phone hadn't died, I could have mentioned how late it is, I thought as I continued my string of non-verbal curses. *Why did I agree to meet him tonight?* There was no way I could have gotten ready in time. *Should I just go, even though I'm not sure he'll show?* I was sweating profusely as I paced my tiny room, riddled with anxiety and completely unable to make a decision.

Realizing that I had already wasted ten minutes in panic, I finally made the decision not to go. *There's no way he thought we had firm plans. His phone died before we confirmed anything. He's not going to show.* My rationalization allowed me to get my breathing and my sweating under control. I climbed back into bed, resumed watching *The Real Housewives of Atlanta*, and sent Eric a quick text for when his phone was charged again, something along the lines of *so bummed we couldn't make it happen tonight, but I still can't wait to meet you.*

At quarter of twelve, my phone rang. It was Eric. "What happened?" He sounded hurt. "You didn't show."

I was immediately sweating again as I offered my lame apology and explained myself. If he had stayed on the phone, I told him, he would have heard me say that the Metro was running slow and it would take me too long to get there. He would have heard me counter with a different day and time for our date. He said he understood, though I could hear the disappointment in his voice. We said goodnight, but my anxiety afforded me little sleep.

The next day, I sent him a text, trying to make light of the situation and letting him know that I was still very interested in meeting him. No response.

Another day came and went, and still no word. We had gone from texting several times a day, every day, to not speaking. *I managed to fuck up another one*, I screamed at myself. *This time I fucked it up before I even met him. Now that takes talent.* The voice in my head knew exactly where to strike to evoke maximum pain. I was a wreck.

Not content to sit back and let another guy just disappear, I messaged Eric. I explained one more time why I hadn't shown up and told him truthfully that I hadn't found anyone quite as funny or attractive as him before. I reminded him that based on the texts he had been sending me before I screwed everything up, it seemed as though he felt similarly about me. I made a final plea to at least meet up in person before deciding it wasn't worth pursuing. Every other guy who had dumped me had at least afforded me that courtesy. Then I waited, not knowing if he'd bother to respond.

Fourteen restless hours later, he responded. *No worries, no worries at all love,* the message began. The weight of the week was immediately lifted. I felt light, happy. His message went on to explain that while he was indeed disappointed, he wasn't about to let something that stupid keep us from meeting. He apologized for his silence but reminded me that he worked full time and went to law school in the evenings, so he occasionally got overwhelmed with work. I was ready to forgive/be forgiven, forget, and give it another try. I also vowed to look impeccable at all times until after our first meeting, even if it meant sleeping in my jeans and waking up early every day to wash my hair. I couldn't be caught off guard again.

That Friday afternoon, as my blood pressure and sleeping patterns returned to normal, Eric texted. He was downtown waiting to pick up a legal brief and felt like chatting. He suggested we pass the time by playing *Words with Friends*, but I reminded him that 1) I was at work, and 2) I didn't have a smartphone. In fact, my phone barely functioned as a phone. At best it was a weapon, something I could throw at would-be muggers. He laughed (via text) and said, *Well, you could tell me more about yourself over drinks.* I immediately replied that I was free and would love to finally meet him.

The rest of the workday was a wash. I couldn't concentrate on anything except my outfit choices. It was early November, but still considerably warm outside, which meant I could wear my brown faux-leather jacket. I owned very few trendy articles of clothing, but in that jacket I felt confident.

I hadn't heard back from Eric, but slipped out of work a little early to rush home and groom. I wasn't about to make him wait on me again. Skipping the gym, I showered and shaved, put on makeup, and threw on a casual, but cleavage-revealing outfit and a pair of earrings I had just purchased the previous weekend. All I needed was a time and a place. I sat on my bed and waited.

At 10:30 p.m., after hours of obsessively checking my phone for missed calls or texts, I resigned myself to the fact that I wasn't going to hear from Eric that night. *Had I read too much into his text?* I wondered. *Or maybe he's just trying to let me know what it's like to wait on someone?* Though I didn't know him well, that didn't seem like his style. Disappointed, I washed my face and got ready for bed.

The next night, I met Kat out downtown, in an area we had frequented in grad school because of its proximity to GW. We stopped in one bar known for very large, very cheap mixed drinks. It was early yet, only 10:30 p.m., and the few people in the bar were standing in front of a flat screen cheering on Oregon State's football team.

Kat and I took the opportunity to chat before the DJ started spinning and the crowd picked up. She told me the most recent tales of government inefficiency and I, of course, filled her in on the highs and lows of my short courtship with Eric. I searched her face for a reaction, but she seemed less than interested. I couldn't entirely blame her, as I had spent the better part of the last few months getting really excited, then really disappointed about James, then JD, and now Eric. Still, as my best friend, it was her job to listen, offer advice, and act like I was always in the right, especially when a guy is a no-show on a Friday night.

Kat was certainly attractive, with a thin, athletic frame, plenty of curves, and large blue eyes adorning her round face. But her focus these days was on her career as a government contracts lawyer, which was thriving. She did very little dating, which made my whining about boys feel even more juvenile.

Shortly after Oregon State's victory, the bar began to fill with people looking to mingle. The tables around us had been cleared to make room for a dance floor, and Ke$ha was telling me to make the most of the night like I was gonna die young. I guessed that if I lived like Ke$ha, I probably *would* die young.

We danced the rest of the night away, and by 2 a.m., we were on the Metro slowly heading to our respective homes.

Lying in bed at 11:30 on Sunday morning, I realized I had absolutely nothing to do that day. I forced myself to get up and go to the gym to kill some time. Afterward, I showered, washed my hair, and put on makeup, just in case Eric happened into my neighborhood again and wanted to see me. He didn't.

The next day was Veterans Day, offering me a reprieve from work, but still no social invitations. I repeated my routine from the previous day and finally decided to text Eric. *Am I ever going to meet you, or are you imaginary?* I asked. I went for a walk as I awaited his response.

Shortly after 6 p.m., he replied. He confirmed that he was indeed real and that he absolutely wanted to meet me, but was super busy. He said he could be free for an hour or two that evening, around 7:30, and asked what I had in mind. Since I had blown our last opportunity to meet, I offered to meet him at a bar in his neighborhood, Silver Spring. It was about an hour away on the Metro, quicker by bus. Unfortunately, the buses were running on a mysterious modified holiday schedule with the departure times merely listed as "more frequent than weekend service, but less frequent than weekday service." That was entirely unhelpful, so I opted for the train.

Realizing I'd have to leave soon, I picked out a good first-date outfit, checked my hair and makeup, and downgraded from my giant work purse to my less-giant (but still Mary Poppins-esque) casual purse. You never know when you're going to need to produce a potted plant or a coat rack.

With ten minutes to spare, I realized that I hadn't specified dinner as part of the date, just drinks. I needed to eat something fast. I couldn't risk getting tipsy; I had to be at my wittiest so I could trick this guy into falling for me. I grabbed a spoon and a jar of peanut butter and had at it, then brushed my teeth for the third time that day.

I arrived at the Metro station just as the train I needed

was pulling away. *Shit*, I cursed to myself. I could feel the perspiration forming on my neck and under my boobs. I began a crossword puzzle, hoping to distract myself, and, therefore, my sweat glands until the next train arrived eight minutes later.

I finally arrived at Silver Spring, a bustling neighborhood just over the DC–Maryland border, an hour later and power-walked my way toward Georgia Avenue, using my hand-drawn map as a guide. Just my luck, it had started raining—not hard enough to need an umbrella, but just enough to transform my hair from perfectly curled to country-music frizz. Adding insult to injury, despite knowing the address, I couldn't find the bar. I found the building—8401 Georgia Avenue—but Quarry House Tavern was nowhere to be seen. After rounding the block, being followed by a chatty homeless man, and stopping in an Indian restaurant to ask for directions, I finally found the place—just around the corner from the building's main entrance, next to the homeless man, and down some shady looking steps. The only sign: the letters QHT above the unlit stairway. I was stressed, nervous, wet, and late.

I walked into the dim bar expecting failure. And then I saw him, sitting alone at a table near the bar in a yellow plaid shirt and tight-fitting khakis, stroking his scruffy beard. Normally, I didn't find the hipster look particularly attractive, but Eric pulled it off perfectly. I couldn't believe that this insanely attractive guy was waiting for me. Then, realizing that it was entirely possible I was approaching the wrong guy, I quickly scanned the area for other lone men. None. This was the guy. What was that I'd said about not wanting to get tipsy? Screw it. I needed a drink.

As I approached the table, he looked up and smiled at

me. I immediately knew this was going to be a great first date. He proved extremely easy to talk to, firing off a litany of unusual questions: What was my favorite board game? How had we come up with our pets' names as kids? And, as we sipped our second drinks of the night, we bonded over our love of Christopher Meloni, both for his work in *Law & Order: SVU* and for his genius comedic performance in the movie *Wet Hot American Summer*. We briefly discussed our career aspirations—his, to be a litigator, and mine, to help underserved communities address their unique health needs—but mostly we just laughed. I had never experienced a first date that was so effortless and easy (if you conveniently forget all the drama leading up to my arrival at the bar), and I was genuinely disappointed when he informed me shortly after 10 p.m. that he had to get home to study.

He offered to drive me back to the Metro station, and I gladly accepted. A block from the station, we were stopped at a traffic light and he turned to me and smiled. *Don't fall for him yet,* I heard the voice in my head cautioning. *You fall for guys too fast. Give this some time.* But I already knew it was too late. I was falling.

That night, I lay in bed restless, reliving every moment of the date—our conversation, the way he smiled at me, his slightly awkward but endearing mannerisms, the way he smiled at me... I barely slept that night.

The upcoming work week was a struggle. Though Thanksgiving was still over a week away, projects began to grind to a halt. My workload was light, but I refused to sit around all day daydreaming about a boy. So I compromised, spending half of each day daydreaming and the other half reading the news online.

Fortunately, Thursday night finally arrived, and I headed to the airport on very important travel: I was flying to Boston for opening weekend of the very last *Twilight* movie. It was a tradition my friends and I started years ago, before my move to Atlanta. I had seen each of the movies, save one, on opening weekend with my friends Laura, Alycia, and Martina. We didn't attend for the acting—I think we can all agree that Kristen Stewart only has one facial expression: disgust. We weren't there for the romance—a man who breaks into a girl's home to watch her sleep is a stalker, not a Romeo. We certainly weren't there for the eye candy—seeing Robert Pattinson with his shirt off made me worry about his health, and, while more attractive, Taylor Lautner's shirtless close-ups always made me feel slightly uncomfortable. We were there for mindless entertainment and an excuse to see each other again. And sure, I related to main character Bella's boy-crazy neuroses better than Laura and Alycia (both married with children), but I never let on that I believed her desire to become a vampire for the sake of her vampire love was rational. I mean, you know, if vampires existed. Which they don't. I'm pretty sure.

On my way to the airport, I got a text from Eric. He wanted to know when he could see me again. After the initial rush of joy, I again found myself thinking, *He's too good for me.* And I knew it was true. I knew my strengths— I could be hilarious, I was friendly, and, given the right clothes and lighting, I was even reasonably attractive. But, as a thirty-year-old who had never been in a serious relationship, I didn't know how to navigate past those first few dates. Eric was funny, gorgeous, smart, ambitious, and far more emotionally mature than I was, despite being six years my junior. Not wanting to show him how excited I was after just one date, I decided to play things cool, which unfortunately in my case meant aloof. I let him know that I'd be out of town and busy that weekend, but that I couldn't wait to see him when I returned.

Riding my text message high, the rest of the weekend was perfect. I packed my schedule with visits with old friends, gorged on Chinatown's most delicious dim sum, allowed myself to believe in love again (or at least vampire love), and went dancing at one of my favorite clubs. I was happy.

Returning home, I was anxious to see Eric again. Unfortunately, his packed schedule of work during the day and classes or studying at night didn't allow time for another date before I found myself boarding the train to Connecticut for Thanksgiving a week later. I had been single for every major holiday of my life. In fact, it had become an unwelcome Thanksgiving tradition for my maternal grandmother, a loving but hardened woman, to ask, "So, have you found anyone you like better than yourself?" It was never in jest; she was serious. I always managed to laugh despite wanting to cry. And, though I knew things were still too new with Eric to mention him this holiday, I let myself wonder if maybe next year I'd have a different response.

Eric and I texted all week. He confessed that he really liked me, more than he should after just one date. Though I felt the same way I couldn't bring myself to tell him, afraid that maybe he'd freak out and disappear. Instead, I deflected with self-deprecation, joking that he only felt that way because I was the only life he currently had outside of work and school. I had two emotional settings when it came to guys: uninterested and completely head over heels crazy. And I wasn't uninterested in Eric.

I returned from Thanksgiving feeling great. I had caught up with two of my high school friends over waffles and hash and spent some quality time talking and playing cribbage with my family. Often, being around my siblings and their spouses in addition to my parents—who were still impressively affectionate toward each other—made me feel lonely and out of place during family gatherings. But, for the first time in my life, I spent a holiday feeling happy and cared about. I couldn't wait to return to DC to see Eric again.

He had evening classes all week, but by that first Friday back in DC I couldn't wait any more. He was exhausted from a busy week, but I convinced him to see me that night. I offered to travel to his neighborhood again so as not to put him out. Knowing how temperamental the universe was, I should have built additional time into my travel schedule. However, I thought I could be in Silver Spring by 6:30 p.m. and suggested a bar that had happy hour specials till 7. At 5:20 p.m., I boarded the train, boob sweat-free and feeling excited. I had timed it perfectly. Until a disabled train on the tracks ahead of us caused a fifteen-minute delay. My train didn't pull into Silver Spring station until 6:30 p.m. I called Eric as I exited the train to let him know that I was still ten minutes away. He, of course, was already at the bar. I could immediately feel the boob sweat forming.

Since it was rush hour, I followed the sea of people off the train and out of the station. Once outside, I realized that I had exited from a different turnstile than I had the last time I was in the area, and I didn't recognize my surroundings. Not wanting to keep Eric waiting any longer than necessary, I approached a confident-looking guy walking beside me and asked him for directions to Georgia Avenue. He smiled and walked me across the street and pointed to my left. "Walk that way for a few blocks and you'll see it," he directed me. I thanked him and began my brisk march toward Eric.

Ten minutes later, I found myself walking along a highway, no buildings in sight. The pit in my stomach told me I was walking in the wrong direction, but I maintained hope that if I just kept walking I'd hit an intersection with Georgia Avenue. After another five minutes of walking and not encountering another pedestrian I called Eric. "I'm at the intersection of 16th and Portal Streets," I told him, hoping it would mean something to him.

"I have no idea where that is," he responded unencouragingly. I tried to maintain my cool as he tried to locate me on a map on his smartphone, since I didn't possess that new-fangled technology. He was unsuccessful. My boob sweat had spread and had encompassed my entire upper body. I knew what I had to do. I had to retrace my steps all the way back to the Metro station and then walk in the opposite direction toward the tall buildings. So much for relying on the kindness of strangers.

I arrived at the bar forty minutes late, well after the end of happy hour, and drenched in stress sweat. He was patiently waiting for me and smiled broadly when he saw me walk in. He looked amazing—wearing a tight purple button-down shirt and a black vest—and if he was annoyed by my lateness, he never let it show. We immediately fell into a great conversation.

After dinner, he offered to show me around Silver

Spring, as I was clearly unfamiliar with the area. Since I hoped to be spending more time there, I figured it was worth getting to know my surroundings. I never wanted to keep him waiting again. Walking past the AFI Silver Theater, a three-screen theater that showed a mix of independent, art house, and classic films, he noticed that *The Fantastic Mr. Fox* was showing that evening. Upon hearing that I had never seen the film, he purchased two tickets for the 9:00 p.m. show, insisting that it was a movie I had to see. To kill time till the movie started, we walked around the shopping district; he took my hand in his. Though it was probably thirty-five degrees outside, I didn't feel anything but happy. Stopped at a traffic light waiting to cross the street, I began to tease him about his hipster clothing, specifically his very tight pants. He laughed at my lame jokes and kissed me there on the corner.

Taking shelter from the cold, we entered the theater at 8:30 p.m. and cozied up to each other at a high-top table in the lobby near the concession stand. He excused himself to use the bathroom, and I pulled the *Express*—DC's free daily newspaper—out of my purse to continue the crossword puzzle I had been working on during my train ride. Engrossed in crossword clues, I didn't see Eric return. He sat down next to me, started reading over my shoulder, and began suggesting answers. With his hand on my thigh, we successfully completed the puzzle together before the movie began.

Once seated in the theater, he returned his hand to my thigh and I placed my hand on his. I'd never enjoyed a movie as much as I enjoyed *The Fantastic Mr. Fox*, mostly because of the constant physical contact with a guy I found irresistible, and partly because of the light-hearted humor of the stop-motion animated film. Throughout the movie, his hand never left my leg and my hand never left his. I was angry when the movie ended, knowing that it meant our evening together was almost over.

We braved the cold and walked back to his car hand in hand. He opened the passenger door for me, and we kissed again. I was secretly hoping he'd invite me to come back to his apartment for the night, but acted content when he said he had to go home and study for the rest of the evening. As much as I wanted to make out with him all night, I admired his commitment to law school. I'm not sure I could have made the same decision, had our circumstances been switched. He drove me to the Metro station, and we kissed again before I forced myself out of his car.

The universe, sensing that I was happy, did what it could to destroy what remained of my night. I walked to the front of the station to find the entrance barred. There were no signs or employees to be found, just a few confused people like myself milling about. I approached one, still grinning like an idiot, and asked if she knew what was happening.

"Do I look like I know?" she snapped.

I decided it was best to change my location. Walking around the building, I finally stumbled across a single sign that read "Track work for the Red Line beginning at 9 p.m. November 30th until closing December 2nd. Station closed. Board shuttle buses ahead." I looked at the sad red arrow pointing vaguely down the street, but saw no sign of a shuttle bus or a Metro employee.

Still smiling, I made my way down the street. Others who had been standing outside the station began to follow me, assuming I knew what to do. Not surprisingly, the lone arrow on the sad little sign was not entirely accurate. Several blocks up and along a side street, I happened upon some Metro employees standing next to even smaller signs demarcating shuttle bus pick-up zones. I waited patiently in the cold for ten minutes for a bus, still feeling invincible.

Not entirely sure where I was going, I exited the bus I had been loaded on at the Fort Totten Metro station—an area of northeast DC I had never explored—when everyone else did. We were told we could catch the next Red Line train toward Shady Grove from there. So, we waited. And waited. And waited. The people around me could sense my good mood, and strangers started to approach me to chat. I made friends with a Metro employee who informed me he would be stuck there all night to supervise the shit show and got to know a seventeen-year-old girl who was planning to attend college to be a police sketch artist. I offered her the sage advice of a low-level government employee: make sure you have a back-up career; this city's expensive. I had a decent salary, lived (with an intolerable roommate) on the outskirts of the city, and still couldn't afford a car and all the parking, insurance, and inevitable repairs that came with it. I had been lucky. Living in major cities my entire adult life meant I never had to take on that added expense.

But that night especially, a car would have come in mighty handy. It took me two hours to get home, but I wasn't fazed. I was in too good of a mood to crack. Adding to my feelings of elation, I discovered a text from Eric, sent sometime during my odyssey, that read, *You make wonderful company, truly.* The universe had finally lost one and I was gloating. Big mistake.

The next three weeks played out like a comedy of errors. The week after our blissful second date I waited around patiently for a call, a text, a carrier pigeon, anything. Eric and I had spoken in generalizations throughout the week—neither of us could wait to see the other—but he was too tired to go out Friday, I was busy Saturday, and he had to study Sunday. Finals were only a week away. Since December is notoriously unproductive in the federal government (everyone scrambles to use up their annual leave before they lose it in January), I whiled away my week reading online news, stretching out the few work tasks I actually had, and daydreaming about a relationship that barely existed.

That week was painful. The days ticked by so slowly, I'm pretty sure Tuesday lasted at least forty hours, and my mind was filling those hours with fantasies. All I wanted to do was show up at Eric's apartment (on time and sweat free), pull him down onto his couch, and not come up for air for days. I had never dated anyone as physically and emotionally attractive as Eric, and the anticipation of the inevitable was killing me.

The next weekend came and went, and still no plans with Eric. At this point, I would have settled for in-person conversation and an inappropriate leg rub, but I was left yet again alone and frustrated. The few texts I received reminded me that this was an extremely busy and important time for Eric, but that he couldn't wait to see me again when finals ended.

Rather than sit at home like some cliché lonely rom-com loser, I spent my weekend apartment hunting. My year lease, and eight-months of captivity with Ray, was almost over. I would soon be free!

That third Sunday in December, I checked out a great 3-bedroom apartment in a high-rise near the Van Ness Metro station in northwest DC, just a few miles north of the city center. Two of the girls were staying, but the girl in the master bedroom was vacating. Her room was huge, with two walk-in closets and its own bathroom, and the two remaining roommates I met seemed fun, interesting, and, importantly, social. In other words, the exact opposite of Ray. After giving me the tour, the girls asked me about my current living situation. We sat on the sun-drenched couch in the spacious living room, and I told them about Ray.

"Why are you living with him in the first place?" the girls asked in unison, astonishment in their voices. I went on to explain the series of events that led to us cohabitating against my will.

The girls were sympathetic and told me they only had one more person coming to look at the apartment before they made their decision, but that they hoped they could help me escape.

Feeling successful, I headed downtown to see the White House Christmas trees. The time between Christmas and Thanksgiving had a unique feeling in the city—solemn and beautiful and wistful—and I was ready to let the beauty of the season wash over me.

The holiday display didn't disappoint. The main attraction, a Fraser fir imported from North Carolina, was decorated in hundreds of lights with a toy train circling its base and fifty-six smaller trees representing the US states and territories encircling that. I walked the path along the perimeter, dodging families and couples. As I stopped in place to take in the scene, an older man stood next to me and began to chat. He was from West Virginia but came to DC every year to see the tree. I was pleased to have a companion who was also on his own, and we spoke about the holidays for a bit. He told me about his children and gushed about his love of the holiday season, and I described my favorite Christmases as a child, waking up to a snow-filled yard and a fire roaring in the fireplace. After ten minutes or so, an older woman approached and grabbed his arm. "Are you ready to go?" she asked.

"My wife," he explained. "She doesn't love the tree as much as I do." He smiled at me as he walked away, arm in arm with his wife. I immediately resented him. I had related to him as a lonely stranger. Instead, he had someone to share the holidays, and his life, with. I watched them retreat into the crowd, then turned to continue my stroll along the path of trees.

The sun had long since set, and as the lights lit up the ruddy faces of the happy strangers around me, I suddenly felt very alone. I had to get out of there. By 8 p.m., I was home and in the shower, washing the city and my disappointment away.

The next day, Eric sent me a message via Gchat (a precursor to Google Hangouts): "What happened last night? Didn't you get my voicemail? I wanted to see you." I immediately checked my phone. No missed calls or waiting voicemails. In the three years I had owned my phone, that was the first voicemail it had decided not to give me. At least, that I knew of. *Seems about right*, I thought bitterly. I replied that I hadn't received a message and would have loved to have seen him, but even as I typed it, it sounded like a replay of our first missed encounter at Buffalo Wild Wings.

The ensuing week was painful. I was lonely and missing this guy I had gone on a mere two dates with. As a thirty-year-old woman with rising estrogen levels, I was impatient to make out with Eric. It didn't help that I still had nothing to occupy my thoughts at work except revisiting Eric's online dating profile. Most of the people I reported to were gone for the remainder of the year. Even the news stories about the impending fiscal cliff that would have drastically contracted the economy were becoming tired and repetitive. I needed something, anything, to keep me busy till the weekend, when I was sure I'd finally get to see (and touch) Eric.

I began that weekend with a quick, casual text to let him know I was thinking of him. When I hadn't heard from him by Sunday morning, I called and left a message explaining that I was free that night, if he wanted a study break. I hoped he was able to read the not-so-subtle subtext. That night, when I still hadn't heard from him, I sent him a Gchat message. Nothing. I was far too frustrated and in need of physical contact to wait another week. Plus, I was leaving for Connecticut the following Saturday for Christmas. I needed desperately to see him naked before then.

Though he had given no indication that he was done with me, the situation was becoming all too familiar. It had only been a few months since JD had told me how much he liked me, and, in the same week, stopped speaking to me. I had promised myself (and my poor friends who had to listen to me bitch and moan about it afterward) that I would never let a guy get away with ghosting me again. If he wanted to dump me, I would make sure to put him through the unpleasantness of at least telling me.

The combination of my self-doubt and the lascivious thoughts racing through my clouded mind meant I was in no way capable of making smart decisions. Harnessing all the restraint of a sex-crazed teenager, I sent Eric a polite, but dramatic email where I basically told him the things I wished I had said to JD—that I was a person who'd invested time and energy in him, and therefore deserved an acknowledgement at the end; that his silence said more about his character than it did about our brief romance.

(Un)fortunately, he wasn't JD and responded to my message immediately with remorse, a little confusion, and much exasperation. Here he was in the middle of balancing his full-time job and law school finals, and the crazy girl he had gone on two dates with was upset that she wasn't getting enough attention. I was officially acting like every annoying rom-com lead character ever.

The difference is that in rom-coms, the guys find this charming. Eric did not.

We spoke a few more times that week after his finals were over, his tone more reserved than in the past, and I mentioned I was free that Friday if he wanted to celebrate. He didn't commit. Nevertheless, I ran home after work Thursday to bake him Funfetti cupcakes (the only cupcakes he liked), just in case.

He never called. I spent Friday, December 21st, the night before my Christmas vacation, crying as I tossed cupcakes one by one into the trash. I was devastated, and not just because seeing cupcakes in the trash goes against everything I believe in.

I wished I could go back in time and try again. I would show up to our dates on time. I would invest in a phone plan with better coverage. I wouldn't overreact and send

Eric dramatic emails. I would work harder to show him I was worthy of his affection. If he would just give me another chance, I would be whatever he wanted me to be. And maybe this time the guy wouldn't just disappear.

THE END OF THE WORLD

December 21, 2012—the Mayan Apocalypse was upon us. The news outlets had spent the better part of the week debunking the end-of-the-world conspiracies. I was mostly ambivalent. As the sun set outside my window, I sat in bed thinking about how it wouldn't really be that terrible if the world ended that night. Sure, it would be sad to never see my friends and family again, but it would be nice to not have to deal with the emotional rollercoaster that was my life. I was ready for a break, permanent or otherwise. Don't get me wrong, I wasn't depressed or suicidal. Just tired and looking for a reprieve.

Over the past few years, and especially of late, I had felt a shift in the overall perspective of my life. When younger, I used to go out with friends, drinking, dancing, playing games, going on spur-of-the-moment adventures, all for fun. Except for the years I had spent in the thick of my eating disorder—which my brain had kindly compartmentalized and stashed away as a foggy, dream-like memory—I had genuinely enjoyed myself and thought often that I led a pretty great life. But, during my late twenties, while I was busy being consumed with self-loathing and insecurity, many of my friends had paired off and started families. I had forged ahead with my life of drinking, dancing, games, and trips. Lately it seemed I was working hard to convince myself that my life was still exciting, rewarding.

In the last few years alone, I had overcome a pretty debilitating eating disorder, and I had picked up and moved myself from Boston to Atlanta—a city where I knew literally no one—all by myself, not even family by my side. I hadn't just survived, I had thrived. I spoke about those years of my life as a triumph. I had shown I didn't need anyone; I could do it all alone. I felt sorry for my female friends who didn't like to travel without their boyfriends or husbands. I laughed to myself at people who were too afraid to move away from their families. I was superior. I was self-sufficient. I was brave. As a single, independent woman in the post-feminist era, the world was supposed to be my oyster. But, as it happens, I don't really care for oysters.

For some reason, my many accomplishments, all hard-earned and self-won, didn't seem to carry the same weight as those traditional milestones reached by so many others my age: marriage, children, home ownership, a subscription to the *Economist*. I was fiercely independent, which felt alarmingly similar to being completely alone.

A few nights before the supposed end of the world and my rejection by Eric, I attended happy hour with my former grad school friends Jess and Miriam, with whom I still occasionally hung out. Jess, one of those people who is always put together and polished, arrived looking haggard and upset. We immediately got a drink in her hand and asked her what was wrong. The three of us had long been dissatisfied with our general career trajectories, but Jess explained that her current workload at a local nonprofit health organization had become untenable, and her boss, unprofessional. Just the week before she had experienced her first panic attack, set off by a confrontational meeting with her boss, and now she was contemplating quitting. As she described her inability to breathe and the embarrassment of having a coworker call her fiancé to come pick her up at the office so she wouldn't have to Metro home in her fragile condition, I realized I was jealous of her. Here she was describing one of her worst moments, and all I could think was if that happened to me, I'd have no one to call. I silently chastised myself for making Jess's situation about me, and made up for it with extra concern, in the form of drinks, for my friend. But the thought was there, festering. *I have no one.*

In reality, that wasn't true. If needed, I had great friends who would come to my aid. But it wasn't quite the same. I was finally ready to admit the one thing single, independent women were never supposed to admit—I was lonely. Unbearably so. I wished I had someone by my side to help me with my impending move from Maryland to my new apartment in DC's Van Ness neighborhood, someone to spend holidays with, someone to physically and emotionally lean on when I had a shit day and just needed support. I had proven that I could do it all alone, but I didn't want to anymore.

For years, I had plastered a smile on my face when friends curiously questioned me about my love life, saying that so-and-so wasn't right for me or I just hadn't found anyone who interested me. But never fear, I assured them, it's only a matter of time. I just hadn't met the right guy yet. I think it made them feel better to know I hadn't given up. It made it easier for them to share their relationship successes with a girl who believed that she'd get her chance eventually.

But my optimism was in the trash next to Eric's cupcakes. I was now the girl who got angry at the commercials for a seniors online dating site because their tagline was "It's never too late for a second chance at love." *A second chance? What if they never found love the first time around?* I would find myself grumbling whenever these ads interrupted my reality TV. And I was growing angrier at Facebook for filling up my feed with updates about the new relationships of acquaintances I found to be annoying or off-putting. *If these unbearable people could find love, why couldn't I?* The question gnawed at me constantly.

That Friday night, December 21st, I sat listlessly in bed watching the John Cusack end-of-the-world movie *2012* while the minutes ticked by. As I watched the ground crumble away and John's fictitious family face setback after setback, I wondered why they fought so hard to survive.

HARDBALL

I was tying my breasts into a sequined, low-cut halter top, getting ready to go out with Kat one Saturday night shortly after Eric faded from my life, when I got a text. *Hey there. How's life?* It was from James. I hadn't spoken to him since that last softball game at the end of the summer. As far as I knew, he had been dating Jaleo Girl that whole time, and I had been distracted by the disappearing acts of JD and Eric.

James and I briefly caught up and then ventured into mild text flirting. I mentioned that Kat and I were going dancing at a new bar in Adams Morgan and invited him to join. He declined, saying he couldn't believe he was turning down an invitation to go out with two beautiful women, but asked for a rain check. The timing couldn't have been better. I had been an emotional wreck since Eric vanished several weeks earlier, and was only venturing out that night because Kat had convinced me that wallowing in self-pity in public with a friend was way better than wallowing at home with a creepy roommate lurking. I had half-heartedly agreed, though I didn't really feel like being around other, functional people. But James's resumed interest hit me right in my fragile ego, filling me with the self-confidence I needed to march into the thick of Adams Morgan, breasts out, and make out with an attractive guy. My heart wasn't in it, but my tongue sure was.

After a night of dancing and making out with strangers, I was confident that I was on the road to recovery. I no longer needed my grape vodka. I was even feeling flirtatious again.

I began accepting social invitations immediately thereafter, and, while snow tubing the following weekend with Kat and her friends at a nearby ski resort, my phone vibrated. James had messaged me.

Wanna bang it tonight?

I read the words several times. *Bang it?* That didn't sound like him. Since he was still in possession of an old flip phone, I assumed he had mistyped. He must have meant *wanna hang out tonight?*

Sure, I replied. *What do you want to do?*

Anything that involves a hot tub and naked women.

Hmm, maybe I hadn't misread that first text. It was about time he took some initiative. I told him to be at my place at 7.

At 7 p.m. sharp, he was waiting for me outside. Usually he picked me up in his beat-up Ford, but tonight he had parked down the street. He had clearly showered and dressed up for the occasion. I could barely contain my excitement. I had fantasized about wrapping my legs around him for months. There was only one problem—Ray, my ever-present roommate till my move to Van Ness at the end of the month, was home watching a soccer match in his TV-watching uniform: an oversized T-shirt and sweatpants.

After a quick walk around the neighborhood in the frigid January air, stalling in the hopes that the soccer match might have ended, I invited James up to my apartment. I immediately regretted that decision. My roommate greeted us by briefly averting his eyes from the TV screen. He didn't even pretend to offer us use of the common areas. I guided James into my bedroom and closed the door. The wall between my room and the living room did little to dampen the sound of the soccer announcer excitedly reminding fans that the match remained scoreless.

James plopped himself down on my bed, not in a come-hither way, but in a I-have-no-interest-in-working-for-it way. My room seemed smaller than usual with him in it, so I crawled onto the bed next to him. He didn't move. He just kept staring up at my ceiling. We chatted awkwardly for a bit, the sound of screaming soccer fans streaming in through the wall.

I knew that if I just pulled myself on top of him, it would happen. But I didn't want that. I wanted James to initiate, to take me. After forty minutes of light chitchat, it was clear that we were never going to make the leap into a physical relationship. James pulled himself up from my bed and explained that he had to get going. We hugged goodbye and he left. I sat back down on my bed and tried to figure out what had happened. Through the wall, I could hear the soccer announcer screaming excitedly that no one had scored that night.

I assumed that would be the end of it with James, another ghost from my dating life. Yet James kept texting.

It seemed that once sex was off the table, we finally found our fit as friends. The tension was gone, and conversation came a little easier. We began hanging out sporadically— watching movies, having drinks, shooting pool. James even felt comfortable enough with me to break out his chewing tobacco and the makeshift spittoon he kept in his truck. While I really, really wish he hadn't, it was nice to know he considered me a close friend. Possibly his only friend. It was also nice to know I hadn't kissed a guy who used a spittoon.

REBOUNDING

I began an after-work routine of going to the gym, prepping a healthy meal, then packing up my belongings while fantasizing about living in a new space where I could put dirty dishes in the dishwasher. My impending move to Van Ness was a nice distraction, and a reminder that life kept going.

As I began to heal, I leaned heavily on my friends for support in the weeks following Eric's disappearance. When recounting the tale of our dalliance over drinks, I always laid the blame for its failure squarely on the universe. How else could anyone account for the hurricane? Eric's dying phone? The wrong directions and train delays? The missing voicemail?

My friends all countered my conjectures with the simple and perhaps obvious fact that Eric and I were incompatible from the start—his busy schedule meant he couldn't make plans in advance; and my lack of a car, and, apparently, internal compass, meant I couldn't be ready to meet at a moment's notice. One astute observer/three-drink philosopher even suggested that by telling myself that Eric was too good for me, I had turned it into a self-fulfilling prophecy. I sabotaged the relationship from the start so that he'd leave before realizing that he really was too good for me. I chose to ignore them all, and, instead, to shake my fist harder at the universe.

Eric was the first guy I had ever truly clicked with on an emotional level. Having never experienced that connection before, I had assumed that once I found it, things would naturally just fall into place. It felt safer to blame our demise on unseen forces than to turn inward and examine the real reasons things didn't work out.

By Valentine's Day, when Eric hadn't made a grand sweeping declaration of love and forgiveness, I knew I had to let go, to find distraction from my loneliness, which still occasionally cropped up. My friend Jess's bachelorette party couldn't have come at a better time. Though her wedding wasn't until May, the party was planned for the long Presidents' Day weekend to accommodate the women who were traveling from out of town.

The party got off to a slow start—we all gathered at Jess's apartment to watch chick flicks which, to my horror, included *The Notebook*, a movie I had prided myself on never viewing. After making it through two hours of formulaic love story with a touch of dementia and a girl who loved to run around in the rain (possibly an early sign of the aforementioned dementia), we changed the tone with *Bridesmaids*. Kristen Wiig had us ready to party as we headed out for the night.

After a delicious dinner at a cozy Thai restaurant in the basement of a rowhouse in Petworth, a mostly residential neighborhood in northwest DC near Howard University, we headed over to U Street to stir up some trouble.

Adorned in classic bachelorette attire—a tiara, sash, and a light-up necklace and ring—Jess, a typically shy girl, couldn't be missed, despite her best efforts to blend in. Guys flocked to her the second we walked into Policy, a local restaurant and bar that turned into a club on weekends. I had created a list of challenges for Jess to complete, ranging from the tame (high-five everyone who wishes you congrats) to the racy (exchange an article of clothing with a guy at the bar). Upon learning that Jess had tasks to complete, groups of men in tight t-shirts surrounded us and asked how they could assist. Strangers are helpful that way.

Surveying the crowd, I picked an attractive guy and pointed to the Buy the Bride a Blowjob Shot challenge. "I will, but you can't expect me to go up to the bar alone and order that. Come with me." He leaned in close enough so that I could hear him over the music. He placed his hand on my lower back as he guided me toward the bar. I immediately knew I'd be going home with him.

We spent the rest of our time at Policy intermittently dancing, chatting—he was a divorced Army Major in town from Richmond—and making out like teenagers. At least I think that's what teenagers do. I mostly filled my high school weekends with *National Geographic* animal documentaries.

With help from the bachelorette party and the many willing men, Jess managed to complete most of her challenges before the lights came on and we were ushered out to the freezing street. "Where do you live?" my Army Major Kevin inquired as he kissed me out on the sidewalk.

"Van Ness," I replied, knowing that probably meant nothing to him. But I quickly remembered that since I had just moved into my new apartment (and away from crazy Ray) the previous week, nonessential items like condoms were still packed away in a box somewhere. I had no idea if the Walgreens near me would be open at 3 a.m. but suspected it wouldn't. "Where are you staying?" I asked when I came up for air.

"The Omni Shoreham." The Omni was a luxury hotel just north of Dupont Circle that hosted numerous celebrities, both in politics and entertainment. I could spend a night there.

At this primitive time in history Uber hadn't made its way to the East Coast and cabs in DC didn't yet take credit cards, so we took the long way home. And just over an hour later, after an extensive Metro make-out session, we stepped into his room, which was lavishly furnished with beautifully woven drapery and a thick, feather-filled duvet. Though we had felt each other up on the way to the hotel, we tore off each other's clothes to see what we were working with.

As an Army Major, Kevin was very fit, though he was not as aggressive as I had expected (and hoped). Still, for a one night stand the sex was good. Kevin was a fantastic kisser and great with his hands. And, when he woke me at 7 a.m. for a blow job, I decided that he had earned it. While the experience wasn't nearly as great as it had been with JD all those months before, in the moment I couldn't think of a better way to thank Kevin for his service to our country.

After a quick nap, he was ready to go again. I checked the clock. 8:15. I was supposed to meet up with the girls at 11 a.m. in Virginia for part II of Jess's bachelorette party—the hangover brunch. If I left now I'd be way too early, so

I climbed on top of Kevin to kill some time.

Afterward, I hopped in the shower to wash off Kevin and the night. I dressed and did a final check to see just how tired I looked. The steam on the bathroom mirror did little to soften the harsh lines under my eyes. I removed as much of my dark eye liner as I could without makeup remover and decided I was as good as I was gonna get. Kevin took my hand and led me through the crowded hotel lobby, past the families excited to explore the city and beneath the extravagantly oversized chandeliers that drenched the marble countertops in light. Standing under the heat lamps several feet away from a valet, we kissed goodbye before I braced myself against the wind and the cold and hurried away.

At brunch I tried not to bring up my one night stand. It was, after all, Jess's weekend. But arriving in the same clothes I had been wearing the previous night with a tired face full of smudged makeup told the story for me. After ingesting some much-needed carbs, I was finally coaxed into telling the PG-13 version. This wasn't the time or place to describe Kevin's fantastic oral skills. I had only just met many of these women. The reaction I received was predictable from a room full of mostly married and engaged women. They all wanted to know if I was going to see him again.

"Not a chance," I said as I took another bite of French toast.

"Why not?" Jess, in her bubble of pre-marital bliss, asked with an eyebrow raised. The others all stared at me, expecting a better explanation than I just needed to get laid to get my mind off Eric.

"He lives in Richmond," I stated, assuming that would

end the conversation.

"So?" The chorus of voices was so optimistic. "Richmond's not that far away."

"I don't have a car," I countered.

"Rental cars are cheap." The women were leaning in, hands on the table as if this was just a minor wrinkle in my inevitable love story with a man I barely knew and had no interest in dating.

I laughed. "I'm not renting a car to drive to another city to see a stranger."

"But don't you like him?"

It was a strange question. "I don't know him. It was sex, and it was good. If he's ever back in town for a night and wants to get laid, he has my number."

The girls seemed disappointed that there wasn't more to it. But for me, the night had been a victory. Even more important than the decent sex was the fact that I had successfully rebounded. I had been able to spend the night with someone without thinking about Eric. Sex with strangers could be self-destructive, but in the right context, it could be therapeutic.

I was healed.

TRIVIAL PURSUITS

My one-night stand with Kevin had injected me with, let's call it enthusiasm for finding a match. So shortly thereafter I dove aggressively back into online dating, which was when I came across Derek's OkCupid profile. Derek was a moderately attractive acquaintance of mine from a rival pub trivia team. Overall his profile was pretty generic, not one I normally would have stopped on had I not recognized the face smiling back at me. But there were no bathroom selfies to sift through. Instead, his pictures were all of him doing normal activities—sipping a beer, awkwardly posing with friends on the National Mall, smiling next to a trivia trophy. After studying his pictures a bit, I decided that his dark features, bushy beard, and knowledge of all things obscure were exactly what I was looking for. I sent him a brief message to acknowledge the fact that we knew each other in real life and to hopefully open the lines of communication.

Though I saw him regularly at Caddie's, the bar where we played pub trivia for rival teams, I didn't really know anything about Derek. I did know that he had a mind for trivia—he played at different bars several nights a week and often won—and he seemed to have a good sense of humor. I wasn't exactly swooning, but he met all my immediate criteria for a crush, so I figured it would be easy enough to focus my romantic attention on him for a while.

With a mission in mind, I began interacting more with Derek each week, needling him when his team got a question wrong and pushing his competitive buttons. Though the interactions were slightly juvenile, they gave me something to look forward to.

It took Derek a few days to respond to my initial online message, but he eventually did. The messaging then continued back and forth, bordering on flirtatious but erring on the side of friendliness. After a few weeks, I realized that I genuinely looked forward to hearing from him and seeing him at trivia each week. But despite the constant online and in-person communication, I had a feeling that if anything was going to happen between us, I'd have to be the one to initiate it. He seemed more than a little timid. My upcoming birthday would provide the perfect opportunity to down a few drinks then force him to either acknowledge his feelings for me or make a very uncomfortable exit.

Derek arrived about an hour into my party—a joint birthday celebration for Kat, me, and our friend Tom, held annually at a low-key bar in the Courthouse neighborhood of Arlington, Virginia. None of the people he knew from my trivia team had yet arrived. Clearly uncomfortable, and not much of a drinker, he parked himself in front of one of the bar's many TVs where he promptly became immersed in the Nats game. I tried to introduce him to other attendees, but he seemed hesitant to interact with new people. I began mingling throughout the room, checking on Derek occasionally to ensure he hadn't left. And, though I had intended to moderate my drinking that evening, to get tipsy but not sloppy, I hadn't accurately accounted for just how many birthday drinks our growing group would spring on me. First it was just beer. Then a vodka soda. Then whiskey. Then cider. Repeat.

Before I knew it, it was the end of the night and my friends were saying goodbye. *Wow, that went by really fast*, I thought. Then, seeing that Derek and my other trivia friends were paying their tabs at the bar, I remembered my plan. I marched up to Derek and asked him if he was ever going to get around to asking me out.

He smiled, replying that he was terrible at reading signals, but that he did, in fact, want to take me out. He promised to contact me the following day to set something up.

I felt amazing as my roommate Lindsey and I hopped into her boyfriend's truck. We were making a much-needed late night stop at Ben's Chili Bowl, a DC landmark located on U Street. We parked in an alley behind U Street, and Lindsey's boyfriend immediately walked over to the nearest dumpster to pee. Realizing that my bladder was uncomfortably full, I walked over to a neighboring car, hiked up my birthday dress, and peed against a brick wall. It was glorious. As were the cheese dog and cheese fries I was inhaling ten minutes later. Right next to a clean, warm restaurant bathroom.

The next day, I woke up around noon with a mild headache. Lying in bed trying to assess the full extent of my hangover, I replayed the night. *That went well*, I thought to myself. *I was well-behaved, kept my hands to myself, and managed to get a date out of it.* As if on cue, the texts started rolling in. My friends seemed very concerned about my well-being, all of them telling me that I was hilarious the previous night but offering no specifics. I racked my aching brain for examples of what they were talking about, but I had nothing. As far as I could recall, I had been the model hostess: polite, accommodating, charming.

Several hours and *Law & Order: SVU* episodes later, driven by hunger, I dragged my tired, but mostly intact body into the kitchen, where I ran into Lindsey. She smiled at me but didn't say anything as she watched me microwave some faux-chicken patties. Not exactly the hangover food I would have liked, but I had planned poorly. Finally, I broke. "So, what exactly happened last night?"

She laughed but didn't seem at all surprised by the question. "You had your hands all over *everyone*." I thought back but couldn't remember touching anyone. She continued, describing my groping of Kat, my trivia friends, softball James and the cousin he brought as a guest, as well as Lindsey's own boyfriend, Steve. I had zero recollection of any of that. Apparently, after chugging my fifth (or maybe sixth?) drink, I had blacked out on my feet, coming to only as the party was winding down and my hands were respectably out of other people's clothing.

I retreated to my room, desperately trying to recall memories from the night before, but I couldn't remember anything from those missing hours. The described behavior wasn't entirely unprecedented; my friends all knew I got handsy when I drank. But the realization that Derek had seen it all hit me hard. No sooner had I started to panic about what I might have said or done to him, when the welcome sound of a text message broke through. *Morning sunshine. How ya feeling?* It was Derek. He was still speaking to me. I immediately relaxed as we traded barbs about the previous night. I was leaving for a girls' trip to Florida a few days later, but lined up a first date with Derek for when I returned.

I spent the rest of the weekend moving slowly from my bed to my couch and back again, mustering up just enough strength to send apology texts to the lengthy list of friends I had molested at my party.

SLIGHTLY-NORTH-OF-MIAMI VICE

Everyone just wants to feel good. I had spent so much of the previous fall and winter feeling despondent and tired, but my night with Kevin and budding flirtation with Derek had reinvigorated me. I suddenly felt alive again, and in need of some fun. So, in early April, less than a week after the birthday party I'm told I enjoyed, I planned to meet my Boston friends Cameron and Sarah in West Palm Beach for a long weekend of drinking, dancing, and lounging in the sun.

The day before my trip, I logged into my bank account to assess just how much money I could safely spend on alcohol in the coming days when I noticed something alarming. I had $87 remaining in my account. I anxiously pored over my transactions, trying to figure out if my card had been stolen, and then I saw it—the transfer of $1,350 to none other than my former roommate Ray's account. Though I had called the bank to cancel my monthly rent transfers the second I was out of Ray's lair, it apparently hadn't gone through. Ray had all my money.

I spent my lunch hour at the bank explaining, then re-explaining my predicament to an associate with a flawless façade and unnatural smile.

"Well, the problem is that you set up the recurring transfer in person." I nodded to confirm. "Therefore it can only be canceled *in person*. The representative you spoke with on the phone didn't have the authority to cancel that for you."

I was stunned. "Then why did the rep last month AND the rep I spoke with over the phone earlier today both tell me the transfers were canceled?" I asked in frustration. I didn't have the energy to point out what a ridiculous policy that was.

"I don't know why they both told you that, but phone representatives are unable to cancel those types of transfers," she repeated, her well-rehearsed smile never cracking. "Would you like me to cancel that automatic transfer for you now?" she asked, as if she was doing me a huge favor.

"Yes." I had wanted to sound exasperated and annoyed, but it came out as more of a pathetic grumble.

"Can I help you with anything else today?" she asked, beaming. I wanted to punch her in the face just to see if she'd flinch.

I shuffled out of the bank, completely defeated. Bank of America had won. Bank of America always wins. I knew then what I had to do. I returned to work, swallowed my pride, and emailed Mansplainer Ray, begging him to send me a check for the money that had accidentally been transferred to his account. I could only imagine the lecture about best banking practices that would soon await me in my inbox.

That evening, as I was stewing in my hatred of Bank

of America, I received a text: *Are you at the beach yet?* It was Derek.

I responded that I was still in town, but that by the time he was at work the next morning I'd be sunning myself with a cocktail in hand while sexy cabana boys fanned me.

Make sure they're not too attractive. I don't want competition. I hadn't smiled all day, but suddenly I was happy. Bank of America couldn't take that from me. Or maybe they could. They seemed like the type of company that would try to monetize happiness. And when they did, mine would probably end up in someone else's account.

The next day I was at the airport by 6 a.m. I reread Derek's text for the thousandth time before turning off my cell phone for takeoff. Though exhausted, I was in a great mood when I entered the hotel lobby and saw my friends waiting for me just a few short hours later. Cam and Sarah were two of my closest friends from Boston. Though we had all gone to BU for undergrad, they were two years my junior and I had only shared one class with Cam, Comparative Vertebrate Anatomy. But when I moved back to Boston after grad school for my first job at a local hospital, I ended up working in the same lab as Cam. We became close friends, and I was then introduced to Sarah, her best friend and roommate.

Cam and Sarah were an odd pairing to say the least. At almost six feet tall, Sarah towered over Cam's petite five-foot-two-inch frame. Sarah had pin-straight hair and both acted and dressed flirtatiously while Cam had curly hair and was more reserved in demeanor and styling. Still, they both knew how to have a good time, and I always enjoyed their company.

Excited to see one another, the three of us hugged, lied to each other about how skinny we'd all gotten, and headed up to the room to change into our bathing suits. Being the amazing people they were, they had already scouted out the pools and checked out the outdoor bar options. I texted Derek at 11 a.m. as I lazed by the water, flirting the only way I knew how—with irony and sarcasm about how he was stuck at work and I was in paradise.

Sarah, Cam, and I spent the day by the pool catching up over frozen Miami Vices—half piña colada, half strawberry daiquiri—which I had to charge to my credit card thanks to Bank of America. After the cursory family, job, boys discussions, we delved into deeper conversation. The Boston Marathon bombing had taken place earlier that week. Patriot's Day, or Marathon Monday, was a holiday in Boston. People across the region came to run, or to cheer or volunteer along the course. Cam, Sarah, and I had all been spectators in the past, cheering for friends and strangers alike. Fortunately, no one we knew had been injured in the explosions. But to hear Cam and Sarah recounting that day made me very aware of how lucky we were to be enjoying each other's company.

Weary from our travels and sleepy from the sun, we decided to take it easy that night. As we walked along the main strip outside our hotel, we spotted an outdoor bar with a sandy floor and cornhole in the back. We pulled up stools next to an older gentleman and attempted to get the bartender's attention. Being the magnet for old men that I am, the man next to me immediately engaged me in conversation.

"My daughter tells me I'm not allowed to just ask people if they're lesbians," he began by way of introduction. I smiled, despite myself. "But then how am I supposed to know if women are gay?"

"I guess you could ask if they're together," I suggested helpfully. "But my guess is that if they're not interested in you, it probably doesn't matter if they're gay or not." *Why do I always engage?*

"So, are you gals here *together*?" He winked at me.

"No, no. We're not lesbians," I informed him. "She's engaged," I said, pointing at Cam, "she's in a relationship," pointing at Sarah, "and I'm undesirable." We both broke into laughter as he shouted across the bar to the bartender that our drinks were on him for the night. Like I said, I have a way with the geriatrics.

We shared a drink in the company of my new white-haired friend before excusing ourselves to play cornhole. It was a calm, relaxing evening under the stars—the perfect way to ease ourselves into vacation.

The next morning, we awoke to a buzzing of phones—people texting Sarah and Cam like crazy. *Are you ok? Are you safe?* We immediately turned on the news. During the night, the Boston police had spotted the Boston Marathon bombers, killing one and pursuing the other through the Watertown neighborhood where he was believed to be hiding out. All of Boston was on lockdown, including the neighborhoods where Sarah and Cam lived.

They each quickly called worried family members and texted concerned friends, then we headed out to the pool with our smartphones so that we could keep tabs on the situation. Many of the hotel staff were wearing Boston paraphernalia that day to show their support for the city. It was extremely touching and terrifying at the same time.

We did our best to relax and enjoy the sun between periodic news updates. Cam brought us up to speed on the wedding planning—Sarah was her obvious choice for maid of honor, and I would be a bridesmaid in her November nuptials—and I finally mentioned Derek. Since Sarah and Cam were both in serious long-term relationships, I sometimes felt silly confessing my most recent crushes, especially since those confessions were always quickly followed by stories of me sitting in the tub with a bottle of vodka after yet another breakup. Still, they always seemed interested in my disappointing love life, and I loved them for it.

Shortly after 5 p.m., we decided to go in and get ready for the night. We had previously decided that Friday night would be our crazy night out on the town, though in the moment, with all that was going on in Boston, we didn't especially feel like partying. We showered and readied ourselves in uncharacteristic quiet, glued to the TV. The police had been going door to door in Watertown but had yet to locate the surviving fugitive bomber.

Sarah and Cam had donned short skirts and sparkly, cleavage-revealing tank tops. After a several-minute struggle, I had successfully squeezed my muffin top into my giant black Spanx-like underpants and looked deceptively good in a hot pink dress and wedge heels. Though we looked ready for a fun night out, we certainly didn't feel it. Suddenly, the TV went black.

"I'm making an executive decision," Sarah said, breaking the silence. "No more news. It's time to dance." She pulled out her iPod and put on Taio Cruz's "Dynamite." We slowly began to dance, reluctantly at first. But by the end of the song, we were singing along and throwing our hands in the air as instructed by Mr. Cruz.

After putting the finishing touches on our makeup and

jewelry, getting the thumbs-up from one another, and doing the final mirror-check, we headed down to have the valet call us a cab. We were told it would be a five-minute wait, so we took seats on the plush couches near the door so as not to tire out our heeled feet. As it happened, a TV across from me was tuned to CNN. A yellow Breaking News banner flashed across the screen, along with the words "Boston Marathon Bomber Suspect in Custody." I jumped up and ran to it to make sure I had read that correctly. Sarah and Cam were right behind me. Images of the Boston PD carrying a wounded man out of someone's backyard were being shown on repeat. They caught him! Bostonians were able to move about in relative freedom again! Cam, Sarah, and I exchanged smiles and hugs.

Finally in the mood to celebrate, we rushed through dinner and walked over to a bar that was known to the locals for its great live music, according to our wait staff. We strutted through the crowded entrance and suddenly became very aware that all eyes were on us. We were far too overdressed for this dive, and too young by at least two decades. We could almost hear the collective pop of the pill boxes as sixty-year-old men reached for their Viagra, and felt the burning stares of the older women who resented our mere presence. But the cover band was great and there was room at the bar, so we decided to stay and feel out the crowd.

Despite our conspicuous presence, the bartenders ignored us in favor of their regulars. As I surveyed the clientele, I noticed the man next to me smiling. He must have been in his late sixties based on the streak of white in his hair and the extreme leathering of his skin. I smiled back and remarked that the band sounded great. He nodded, got the bartender's attention, and asked me what I wanted. If only it was that easy with guys in my general age range.

Since Cam and I had just celebrated birthdays, we ordered a round of birthday cake shots. I thanked my new friend as my girls and I attempted a quick retreat, but I was a beat too late in turning my back to him. Before I could escape, I was engaged in conversation. Or, rather, he was talking at me and I was expected to listen politely. I smiled and commented minimally, while Cam and Sarah sent me furtive looks. Conversation inevitably turned to the big news of the day—the capture of the Boston bomber.

"It's a good thing they caught him," my new friend was saying. "Those Arabs have no business attending our schools and living in our communities." I had almost forgotten I was vacationing in a red state.

I immediately became argumentative, explaining that "Arab" is an umbrella term that can't be used to describe the small group of Islamic extremists dead set on destroying America. I further explained that the Boston bombing suspects were not from the Middle East and were, in fact, Chechen. He stared at me, clearly not expecting to meet an outspoken liberal in his local bar, and possibly unaware of what "Chechen" meant. I smiled, thanked him again for the drinks, and fled to a distant area of the bar with Cam and Sarah in tow.

We parked ourselves next to an older couple who seemed friendly enough. The band was covering a recent LMFAO song, but no one was dancing. "Do you know of any bars that have dancing nearby?" we asked the couple. The woman eyed us curiously, probably wondering if we had ended up there as a joke.

She smiled politely, looked us up and down, and replied, "There is one bar up the street that has the kind of dancing I think you're looking for." I felt as if I was being scolded by my mom for being too slutty. She gave us the name of the bar and we downed our drinks and bolted for the door, the gazes from the dirty old men burning holes through our clothes as we fled.

"I feel like I need a shower," Cam whispered when we were safely outside. I suddenly had a much greater appreciation for sleazeballs my own age.

Walking up the street a few blocks, we knew we were in the right place before we saw the sign for the bar. A combination of well-dressed and cheap-looking men and women in their twenties and thirties were streaming into the darkened building ahead, neon light escaping every time the door opened. I heard the opening refrain from "This Is How We Do It" and ran inside to join the party. We had found our people. The drunken leers from this group didn't make us feel so... dirty.

The music was a solid mix of pop and hip-hop, and as I sang along to Usher's "Yeah," I felt two strong hands grab my hips. I danced my way around until I was face to face with my new dance partner and was pleasantly surprised by the perfect dimples smiling back at me. Though very toned and wearing a muscle tee, I didn't get the sense he was a meathead.

"Are you Jewish?" he leaned in and asked over the music. I assume that's what passes for a pickup line in Florida.

I put my hands on his chest. Rock hard. "Yes," I fibbed. It wasn't a total lie, but it certainly wasn't the truth. My dad was Jewish, as my curly hair and surname could attest, but my mom had raised me and my siblings Catholic. Except for my mom, however, none of us was practicing.

My new friend, Nathan, and I spent the next two hours dancing, talking, and groping. Cam and Sarah, as the amazing people they were, left me to enjoy Nathan and were rocking out together near the bar. We met up again as the lights came on and the music stopped, and Nathan kindly offered to drive us all back to our hotel.

We hesitated at the thought of getting in a car with a strange man. Silently, we did the math. There were three of us and one of him. Also, our feet really hurt. We agreed, and Sarah, Cam, and I loaded ourselves into Nathan's sedan. Conversation was rambling and as unfocused as my eyes.

Ten minutes later we were all walking through our hotel lobby, Nathan by my side. I told Cam and Sarah to head up to the room so I could say goodbye to Nathan in private. The second they were out of sight, he took my hand and led me toward the doors of the pool patio just past the lobby.

"Damn, it's closed," I remarked as I saw the velvet rope strung between two stanchions in front of the French doors. Checking to make sure the security guard stationed in the lobby wasn't watching, Nathan stepped over the rope and pushed on the forbidden door, as if knowing it would open. He held the door for me as I slipped outside, feeling like a total badass.

The patio was aglow in a bath of soft purple and green lights, making it look more like a secluded grotto. Water was steaming off the top of the pool and hot tub, creating a thin fog around the deck chairs. The sound of the waves lapping at the beach was audible in the distance, and the sky was full of stars. It was by far the most romantic setting I'd ever personally known. I should also reiterate that I was drunk.

Still holding my hand, Nathan pulled me toward the hot tub. We sat at the edge, our feet dangling in, and chatted for a bit. Had this been a date, it would have been charming and romantic. But it wasn't. I was drunk, sleepy, and only in town for a few days. I wasn't sure how long I was supposed to sit there listening to Nathan describe the details of how he had started his own law practice or the legal trouble his brother had recently gotten into. After what I thought was an appropriate amount of empathetic listening, I kissed him. That shut him up.

Before I knew it, Nathan had disrobed and was standing in the hot tub naked. He looked good. He was broad in the shoulders, narrowing at the waist, with a six-pack and very defined muscles leading down his abdomen. Standing between my legs, he was kissing me and sliding my dress further and further up my thighs.

I was suddenly very aware of the fact that the patio was surrounded on three sides by hotel rooms, all with balconies overlooking the very hot tub that I happened to be fooling around in. I had a choice: I could either call it a night and walk away from one of the most physically perfect men I'd ever seen, or I could have sex with a handsome stranger in a hot tub, possibly under the watchful eyes of pervy hotel guests. Perhaps it was the desire for a good story, or perhaps it was the intense chlorine fumes, but I chose the latter.

With my dress halfway over my head, I remembered my giant black underpants. I hesitated briefly, but as Nathan raced to help me out of my clothes, he didn't seem to notice or care that half of my torso was compressed in a heavy, spandex casing.

I made no effort to remove my Spanx as we continued making out in the water. We could be caught at any moment. And, if pursued, I didn't want to end up running through the hotel lobby completely naked. The underpants were staying on.

I wrapped my legs around Nathan, and he somehow managed to push my spandex chastity belt to the side. This was clearly not his first interaction with women's shapewear. The water splashed around us as we moved, soaking the clothes we had taken no care to discard on the cement just along the perimeter of the hot tub. Though it turns out sex in a hot tub, or maybe just in torso-constricting underwear, isn't great, I felt completely satisfied by the experience.

Nathan lingered in the tub, trying to stroke my hair and kiss me, but my exhaustion had hit hard, as had my fear of being caught by the security guard. We were literally right next to the hotel lobby guard station. I climbed out of the now-calm water and threw on my soaking dress, eyeing the patio doors as Nathan lazily pulled on his clothes. Acting as nonchalantly as possible, Nathan held my hand as we strolled through the lobby, past the guard; I was soaking wet and clutching my bra and purse to my chest in my free hand. We said goodbye to each other at Nathan's car, and he asked for my number. I told him I didn't see the point but gave it to him anyway.

At 3:40 a.m., I strolled into our hotel room. The lights were on, and Sarah and Cam were sitting up in bed, arms crossed. "We saw you," Cam said, her tone a combination of angry and amused. "We saw you in the hot tub."

There was nothing I could do but laugh. They probably weren't the only ones who saw me.

"Did you have sex? In the hot tub?" Sarah seemed more amused by the evening's events than did Cam.

With my back to them, I worked to wrangle myself out of my wet dress. "Yes," I said with a smile, though all they could see was the back side of my Spanx.

Sarah, seeing that I was carrying my bra, asked, "Wait, did you put your underpants back on after you were done?" She was clearly wondering why I would have maneuvered my wet body into shapewear that's difficult enough to wriggle into when I'm dry.

"Nope. We had sex *around* my underpants," I said and laughed again. I was already enjoying telling the story. The night had totally been worth it.

I grabbed my pajamas and headed to the shower. As I closed the door, I heard Sarah's voice. "I guess I won't be going in the hot tub tomorrow."

We spent the next day on the beach, intermittently sleeping and enjoying the warmth of the sun as we jumped through the gentle waves. That evening we enjoyed a casual dinner outside at a bar just a few blocks from our hotel. The smell of sea salt and algae blended into a relaxing perfume that infused my body and produced a sense of tranquility. The sunset cast the entire boardwalk in hues of pinks and purples. I felt warm, relaxed, and completely content. I loved everything about the beach.

The buzz of my phone interrupted my revelry with notification of a new text. Thankfully, Cam and Sarah were studying the drink menu intently and didn't notice me lunge at my phone pathetically. I smiled expectantly as I opened the message, assuming it was from my DC crush Derek.

Do I get to see you tonight? I was confused. Derek knew I was away for the weekend. I then noticed the sender's name: Nathan (bar, FL).

I was irrationally angry at him for not being Derek, and it was obvious in my reply. *No. Not gonna ditch my friends for a guy on our last night together.* I immediately felt like a bitch and tried to soften the reply with a follow-up message. *I had fun though. Thanks again.* He then asked if he could see me again, and I reminded him that I was leaving the following day.

I'd be happy to fly you back here sometime. Are you free at all next month? I was staring at my phone, trying to determine if that was a line or a genuine offer. I didn't really have any desire to see him again, but if it was a real offer, I wondered, would it also extend to my friends?

As I stared at my phone, mouth slightly agape, Sarah knew something was up and casually asked, "Who are you texting?" Her voice indicated that she knew it was a boy.

"No one." I was obviously lying. She grabbed my phone and read the message.

"Holy shit. He wants to fly you back here? Dude, those must have been some amazing undies."

FRIEND ZONE

Though I had known Derek before we started flirting, I could feel my nerves take over as I stood on the corner outside the Metro waiting for him to arrive for our first date. Derek was on the shorter side, probably about five foot seven with an average build. When I first met him, he was clean-shaven, but recently he had started growing a beard. He dressed as most guys in DC dressed when not at work—in a plaid button-down shirt with jeans—and wasn't the kind of guy you notice walking down the street. But he was funny and smart, and what little I knew of him I liked.

Despite knowing each other, we had never spent any time alone together before. And the first twenty minutes or so of conversation epitomized the awkwardness of two people who didn't really know how to interact outside of a group setting. Anyone watching would have known we were on a first date. But, once inside the Newseum, an amazing museum in downtown DC focused on the history of news and journalism, we found our groove. Conversation about the various displays easily gave way to conversations about our lives. We discussed the Great Depression and the Real Housewives. We viewed satirical news clips and learned everything we had ever wanted to know about presidential pets.

Three hours later we emerged on the street, still engaged and not quite ready to go home. Derek suggested we grab some food, and I eagerly agreed. Conversation continued to flow easily, and though I don't remember what we discussed, I remember laughing. A lot.

We both lived north of the city center along the Metro's red line—he in Bethesda, me in Van Ness—so we began our trek home together. I was disappointed that the date had to come to an end but sensed he had enjoyed himself as much as I had. Just before my stop, he thanked me for encouraging him to ask me out, then he got up to walk me to the train door. I surprised him when I kissed him on the lips before exiting the train, but I saw him smile as he walked back to his seat to continue his journey north to Bethesda. I smiled, too, and the people near me on the escalator gave me a wide berth.

We texted every day after that, often first thing in the morning and late at night. I knew myself well enough to know that I tended to get carried away when it came to guys I actually liked, so I tried to temper my enthusiasm when telling my friends about our date. "I think it went well," I would say. Or, "So far we seem to have a lot in common, but who knows. It's only been one date." Inside, I was a teenage girl jumping up and down. Outwardly, I was playing it totally cool.

Derek suggested the zoo for our second date. I couldn't have been more thrilled. Not only was the zoo one of my favorite places in the city, but after being ghosted by JD the previous summer, I was determined to spend a day at the zoo on a date with a guy I was into, to show those animals that I could pair off too.

It was the perfect day except for one thing: every time I inched closer to Derek to read a plaque or get a better view of an animal, he took a step away. By the end of the day, I made a silent game of trying to sneak up on him to see if I could get within his bubble of personal space. But he was on high alert, weaving around strollers and people on cellphones to stay a foot away from me at all times. I would have been impressed if I hadn't been so disappointed.

As we emerged back on the city streets, we found ourselves discussing our future plans. It was the first real conversation we'd had without one of us making a joke. Honest, thoughtful conversation with someone I didn't know well made me feel awkward. I was more comfortable making a self-deprecating comment than sharing my serious hopes or desires, but with Derek it felt easy.

He offered to walk me back to my place, just twenty minutes north along Connecticut Avenue. But as we walked, he conspicuously kept his hands in his pockets though it was a beautiful, sunny May evening. When I invited him up to my apartment, hoping for a quick make-out session, he awkwardly mentioned that he had to go home and do laundry. I quickly kissed him goodbye, more confused than before, and watched him walk away. Was he interested in me? Was he uncomfortable around me? I had no idea.

I recounted the date for my trivia friend, Maggie, who was well acquainted with Derek. "He's terrified of you," she offered. "You're forward and sexual, and he doesn't know what to do with you." Though I wasn't thrilled with that answer, I embraced the idea because it supported my preferred theory that he was interested in me.

For our third date, we went to a Sunday matinee of *Iron Man 3*. I placed my hand nonchalantly in my lap, close enough for Derek to grab a hold of, should the mood strike.

It didn't.

Afterward, he suggested frozen yogurt at a place mere blocks from his apartment. It had started sprinkling outside, so I opened my umbrella and offered him refuge underneath. Though he tucked his head beneath, he kept his body as far from me as possible, jutting out in the rain. When we arrived at the fro-yo place, his body was needlessly wet, and I was feeling dejected. We chatted casually as we enjoyed our yogurt, and before we left, he checked his phone.

"Ohh, it looks like the power went out at my apartment. My roommate just texted." I looked out the window. It was barely drizzling. I wanted so much to believe him, but I couldn't help but think that that was his way of making sure I didn't invite myself back to his place.

He walked me back to the Metro station, and I leaned in to kiss him goodbye. He made no effort to kiss me back, but also didn't resist. I really enjoyed spending time with him, but I was also attracted to him and was hoping for more than a peck on the lips by date three.

Maggie once again reassured me that he was just nervous about getting physical with me. If I was forward enough and led the way, he'd be sure to follow. She had known him longer than I had, and since I wanted to make out with him, to see if this was even worth pursuing, I chose to believe her.

For our next date, Derek suggested that we meet up after work the following Friday at a bar in Woodley Park, near the zoo, for happy hour. I countered with an offer to come to his apartment to hang out, maybe play a board game (not a euphemism, we both really enjoyed board games). He responded that he didn't have any good games and that meeting at the bar was easier.

I tried hard to ignore the obvious signs, but I knew something was up. So when he greeted me with his usual friendly smile outside the bar, I was thrown. We sat and chatted over dinner, easy and funny and light. He caught me up on his work woes and told me about his plans to move to a new apartment. And then, after dessert, he said it. "I love hanging out with you, I just don't want to date you. But can we please still hang out?"

He said some other things, trying to soften the blow, but I didn't hear any of it. I went into autopilot, assuring him that of course we'd still be friends, continue hanging out. It was smart that he didn't want to date me because then we might not end up as friends. And who didn't want more friends? "Friends" was the word of the night, and I sounded like a *Sesame Street* character reinforcing its value.

We Metroed back north together, joking about trivia and the various events we were sure to enjoy as friends. Just friends.

As soon as I exited the train at Van Ness and made sure my back was to him, my smile faded. I texted Kat: *So, Derek doesn't want to ruin our friendship with sex. Too bad. That's my preferred way to ruin a friendship. Also, fuck him. Oh wait, I can't.*

As much as I wanted to be mad at Derek, I had to

respect him for breaking up with me. In person, no less. I appreciated that and wondered to myself if there was a way to screen future suitors for breakup intelligence. Ghosters need not apply; I only wanted to get dumped by the best.

THE SET-UP

You really find out what your friends think of you when they offer to set you up with someone they know. Shortly after my relationship with Derek fizzled, I found out that some of my friends don't like me very much.

First there was Dennis.

One week post-Derek I was feeling pretty dejected. But, in typical Jana fashion I was putting on my biggest smile and laughing with him at trivia as if him not wanting to screw me was the best news I'd ever heard.

Three weeks later, though my face still hurt from all the forced smiling, my ego was finally beginning to heal. I attended a barbecue at the new home of my friends Ian and Gabby in the suburbs of Reston, Virginia in the hopes of meeting new people. Drinking away what remained of my sorrows, I laughed with friends, old and new, about my effortless ability to repulse men. Everyone was drunk enough to find me hilarious, so I continued my one-woman stand-up routine. *I'm so lonely.* Laughter. *Men find me repulsive.* Claps and nods of approval. *I'm going to die childless and alone.* Gasps for air. I was on a roll.

Somewhere in those moments of self-deprecation Gabby decided that I would be a perfect match for her friend Dennis.

"He's hilarious," she slurred over her seventh glass of wine.

That was all the endorsement I needed. "If he's funny, tell him I'll sleep with him." I hadn't intended for her to text that, but I didn't have enough control of my limbs to stop her.

He responded immediately that he'd like to meet me. Because who wouldn't want to meet the girl who promises sex in exchange for a good joke? In the back of my mind, I felt a smidge of satisfaction that at least someone out there wanted to sleep with me. Just not Derek. Gabby gave Dennis my number, and we decided to meet the following weekend.

The date got off to a bad start. Dennis arrived forty-five minutes late. I cut him some slack since he had traveled to DC all the way from Baltimore to meet me. Sadly, the date didn't improve with his arrival. Almost immediately he brought up that he was a guitar player "in a band." *Ugh, here we go*—my knee-jerk reaction. Unless he could play the guitar with his tongue or he'd mastered the upright bass, I wasn't impressed. Most guys on online dating sites touted their ability to play the guitar as if it was a rare skill that all women were seeking. In reality, it was as ubiquitous as pictures posed with exotic animals or claiming to be "really into hiking."

Recognizing my prejudice, I tried hard not to hold his musicality against him since we had only just met. Plus, he had suggested the date activity—bowling at Lucky Strike, a trendy bar/restaurant/bowling alley in Chinatown. I appreciated any guy who could make plans.

Our first game was awkward. His sense of humor was mostly derived from quoting shows I had never seen, such as *Entourage*, then explaining why the jokes were funny. Though the company was proving disappointing, I was bowling surprisingly well for me, breaking a hundred in my first game. In celebration of my accomplishment, I began to dance to the Lady Gaga song being pumped in over the sound system. Almost immediately, I felt arms around my waist and the protrusion of a penis. Dennis was grinding on me in the middle of our well-lit alley. It felt as though every pair of eyes in the room was trained on me and the assault taking place on my hip.

I quickly pulled away and began bowling our second game. Unfortunately, dancing is reflexive for me. I don't often think about it, I just start moving. And every time I broke into dance to celebrate a well-bowled frame, Dennis and his penis found me. I dodged and weaved, avoiding his advances the best I could, and managed to pull out a win in game number two despite the molestation.

We returned our shoes and were preparing to leave when V.I.C.'s "Wobble" began to play. My hips were moving, and I stopped briefly to assess my options: 1) leave Lucky Strike and be one step closer to ending the date, or 2) stay and dance to this addictive song but prolong the date. Mentally, I was ready to leave, but ultimately, I was powerless to resist the dance. Dennis noticed my moves, his fingertips searching for my waist. I quickly scanned the room and noticed a group of four women, dressed in jeans, heels, and a variety of sequin tops, dancing by the bar. "I'm gonna go dance with them," I said without waiting for a response. He stood there watching as we danced, probably wondering what to do with his crotch.

After my little dance party, Dennis walked me to the Chinatown Metro. I was angling for a quick goodbye, but he smiled and suggested that we go dancing, since I clearly enjoy it so much. "It'll be fun. Just you and me. Dancing." He began to gyrate his hips. I knew what he was getting at. He was hoping to get laid. And, to be fair, sex had already been offered via text. However, his jokes had been subpar, and our senses of humor were drastically different. I had promised sex in exchange for a good laugh. I would have settled for a clever pun. Even a humorous limerick. I don't put out for guys who only think they're funny. It just encourages them.

I declined his offer to hump my leg under the guise of dancing and attempted a friendly hug goodbye. But I was too slow. His open mouth found mine. Well, at least it found part of my mouth, part of my upper lip, and the tip of my nose. It was wet, sloppy, and lasted far too long. I politely waited till the Metro escalator whisked me out of sight before I wiped off my face.

As had become the norm, Metro was doing repair work on the tracks that weekend, so trains were infrequent. I boarded the train that was sitting there on the tracks, knowing that it wouldn't depart for another ten minutes. I didn't care. I was happy the date was over. I must have been smiling to myself because a minute later an attractive man in a Metro uniform approached me. He told me he liked my smile and asked if I wanted to ride up front with him. I did.

Metro regulations forbade me from riding with him in the conductor's booth, but I stood next to it as he drove. I sadly learned that he couldn't just bypass all the stops in between Chinatown and my station, Van Ness. But the ride was quite pleasant. I told him about my terrible date in between station announcements, and he got my number before I exited at my stop.

My Metro Guy worked nights and kept irregular hours, so we never did end up connecting for a date. But at least the night with Dennis hadn't been a total waste.

And then there was Jesse.

The same week as the Reston barbecue, I was hanging out at Quincy's Bar, well north of the city in Gaithersburg, Maryland with teammates from a co-ed rec softball league I had joined earlier that summer. We had just won a doubleheader and were celebrating with $5 Miller Lite pitchers and $2 tacos when a semi-cute guy with bleached blonde hair pulled up a stool next to me and held out his hand in introduction.

"Oh, yeah, this is my friend Jesse," explained my teammate Kelly. "I invited him tonight because I wanted him to meet you." She said this loudly enough for the whole table to hear, then went back to eating her tacos while I attempted to figure out just how sweaty I looked. From the taste of salt on my upper lip, I assumed very.

The entire team stared at Jesse and me as we attempted to flirt, me in my oversized red jersey with the name Turd Ferguson in big yellow letters across my back, he in his slightly too-snug T-shirt, jeans that were ripped at one knee, and gauges in his ears. It felt like a disaster in the making, but my team loved every awkward second of it. This evening was going to be fodder for jokes well into the future, I just knew it.

When I finished my tacos I excused myself to the bathroom so I could assess myself in the mirror and wash the film of sweat off my face. My teammate and trivia friend Maggie, who always drove me back to the Metro after games so I wouldn't have to take the bus, was packing up to leave when I returned to the table. Assuming I'd be joining her as I always did, I grabbed my gym bag and began searching for my wallet. "I just need to leave some cash. Then I'm good to go."

"Ohh, uhh, I can't drive you tonight. I need to get home." She seemed uncomfortable and fidgety. She was looking around at my teammates oddly, as if for reassurance.

"Jesse can drive you home," our team captain Aaron chimed in, grinning. "We already asked."

It was clear this crude scheme had been hatched while I was in the bathroom. My team was great at scheming, but they needed some lessons in lying.

To Maggie's credit, she waited until I confirmed that Jesse could, in fact, drive me home before she left. I hadn't been funny or charming, and I certainly wasn't dressed to kill. The fact that he still seemed interested was enough. I had to take what I could get.

The car ride home was informative. I found out Jesse worked as a server in a restaurant nearby and lived at home with his parents in Rockville, a city about ten minutes north of the apartment I had shared with Ray. He had been fired from his previous job as a server for telling off the manager. He had blonde hair, pale skin, and extremely blue eyes. He was so not my type.

So, of course, we made out in the car before he dropped me off.

My first date with Jesse, scheduled for the following week, started out slightly uncomfortable. We had absolutely NOTHING in common—until we started drinking whiskey. Suddenly we were laughing and having a great time. I have no idea what we talked about, but it seemed hilarious. I drunkenly agreed to see him again, but as a server his schedule was constantly changing, so we couldn't nail down a specific time. We made out in the Bethesda Metro station while we waited for our trains— mine to take me back to my apartment in Van Ness, and his to take him back to his parents' house, I assumed before curfew.

After several attempts to get together again, Jesse and I finally managed to meet for lunch the following Thursday, my weekly telework day. We met at the Potbelly Sandwich Shop, a popular chain in the DC metro area, down the street from my apartment since I only had an hour to spare. Conversation was difficult without drinks in our hands, and I immediately knew I didn't want to date him further. But he was still moderately attractive in an unusual way, and we were only a few blocks from my apartment. I lamely brought up the fact that I lived nearby, and without missing a beat he asked if he could see my place. Before my lunch break was over, we were in my apartment having sex. And not just any sex. Really. Good. Sex. Though I knew I didn't want to date him, I decided to keep him around for a little while longer.

I also discovered a bonus of hooking up with someone I wasn't interested in during my lunch break—I could legitimately kick him out immediately after. I didn't have to chill in bed with him and attempt conversation. I was back on the clock, so I helped him find his clothes and one of the ear gauges he lost in my sheets, walked him downstairs, kissed him goodbye, and got back to work. I didn't even have to walk him to the Metro. I could have gotten used to that. Unfortunately, the next week he got fired yet again from his serving job and took a new daytime gig. Since I had no interest in spending evenings with him, when he might want a meal or conversation, our "relationship" quickly faded.

Finally, there was Josh.

Around that same time, I got a strange request from Kat. Her coworker, Regina, had a friend who was requesting my phone number. He and I apparently had met back in March at Regina's St. Patty's Day Party. It didn't bode well that I couldn't remember this guy, but I was still trying to prove to myself that I could be desirable in the wake of so many failed relationships. I told Kat to pass along my number.

Josh and I enjoyed a great first date—dinner and bar games on H Street, an up-and-coming neighborhood packed with bars and restaurants in northeast DC. But I couldn't tell if I had a great time because of Josh's company or because I just really liked playing indoor mini golf in a bar. On the second date, Josh started to open up and let the strange out. No matter what I said during that date, he acted as though he was genuinely amazed by me. There was no way I was as interesting as he made me out to be.

When I mentioned that I had recently started as a weekly volunteer at the zoo and a monkey had already peed on me, his enthusiasm was off the charts, "Wow, you volunteer at the zoo? That's such an incredible commitment. Most people can't give up that much of their time. How selfless." I didn't volunteer because I was selfless. I volunteered because I loved animals, and, to some degree, manual labor.

After mentioning my very brief stint writing a humor column in the BU paper before being asked to resign, Josh leaned in, eyes wide, and took my hand. "Really? You were fired from the student paper? You must have been a really influential writer to evoke such strong reactions from people." Wrong. I was just a novice writer who was more offensive than interesting.

The interest Josh showed in my nail polish color was unsettling. "That's a really great color on you. Why did you choose orange? Is it significant to you? Do you always wear this color?" He stared unblinking, eagerly awaiting my reply.

His intense eye contact made me uncomfortable, so I broke the stare to examine my nails. "Uhh... I have no idea. It was on sale? I'm a nail biter. I try to keep them polished so I don't chew on them as much," I offered, unsure of what he was hoping to hear.

He looked at me, true concern on his face, and placed his hand on my arm. "Thank you so much for sharing that with me. Nail biting can be hard to talk about."

As strange as the conversation was, he was still the best of the odd assortment of guys I was currently seeing. He had a good job, working as a lawyer in Baltimore. He was attractive enough—average height, strong build, bald head, brilliant blue eyes, a nice smile, tailored clothes that fit him perfectly. He lived on his own. And, importantly, he hadn't yet pushed his crotch against my leg. I hoped that if I willed it hard enough, Josh's intensity would win me over—I'd just wake up one day head over heels in love with him, opening up about all the secrets I kept deep inside. Even deeper than my nail-biting habits. Like how I don't wash my hair every day or how I have plantar fasciitis and therefore wear orthotics in my shoes. Serious stuff.

Since he had come to see me in DC twice, I finally made the trek to visit him in Baltimore for date number three. He greeted me at the Amtrak station with a short kiss. We walked around the waterfront downtown, the smells from the various restaurants overlooking the pier mingling in a delicious, if slightly fishy aroma. We then hopped a water taxi to Federal Hill, a quaint neighborhood with unique shops and restaurants, and toured the historic district. We ended up at a crab place right on the water. It was amazing to sit at the edge of the harbor on a warm summer evening, cracking crabs as the sun went down. If I had been with someone I was really into, it would have been the perfect date.

Even though I still wasn't especially feeling the chemistry, we went back to his place after our feast to fool around for a bit. I crossed my fingers that the make-out session would make the trek to Baltimore worth it. I had no idea what I was in for.

Not even five minutes in, he began slowly and deliberately tracing the outside of my lips with his tongue, then gradually moving outward along my cheek in wet circles. My immediate reaction was to gag, but I stifled the reflex and repositioned my mouth over his to discourage the behavior. As he moved down and began kissing my neck, I was able to discreetly wipe his saliva trail off my face.

With him sucking on my neck and his hands respectfully over my clothes, I started to consider the possibility of sleeping with him. But something moist and unpleasant interrupted my thoughts. He was once again assaulting my face with his very wet, very meticulous tongue. I had made out with many a terrible kisser before, but none who seemed so committed to such a repulsive move. He was clearly into it though, moaning a little while I closed my mouth tight and struggled to breathe through my nose. I didn't have the heart to tell him how disgusted I was.

Instead, I once again tried to kiss him as a normal person does, making a contented sighing noise to indicate that that was my preferred method of kissing. But it was no use. He was going to continue to lick my face whether I wanted it or not. I had lost my desire to find out what the sex would be like and found myself staring at the digital clock on the desk behind him as he made out again with my neck. If I caught the 10 p.m. train back to DC, I could meet up with a group of friends who were going dancing that night on U Street.

The next time his tongue brushed my face, I pulled away.

"Oh, look at the time," I said, acting as if I hadn't been staring at the clock for the past few minutes trying to decide how to gracefully extract myself.

"Hmm, almost 10," he said dreamily as he tried to reconnect with my lips.

"Yeah, I know. I should probably get going. I don't want to risk missing the train."

He looked confused. Given all the moaning and face-licking on his part, he was ready to go, and it very clearly showed. I got up from the couch to use the bathroom, mostly to wipe down my face, but also to allow him a few minutes to cool down.

After a very brisk walk, we made it to the train station with a minute to spare. I gave him a closed mouth kiss goodbye and boarded my train without looking back. I had packed an emergency change of clothes on the hunch that I'd need to bail on Josh and join up with my friends. I pulled on a tight, low-cut sleeveless shirt in the bathroom when I arrived at Union Station in DC and switched my sandals to heels in the cab. By midnight I was sipping a drink and dancing with my friends.

When I inquired among the group if face-licking was more common than I was aware, they all seemed appropriately disgusted.

"Why didn't you just ask him to stop? Tell him you didn't like it? Now he probably thinks you love getting your face licked." My friends may have had a point.

"But how do you tell a guy, mid make-out, that he's a terrible kisser without bruising his ego?" I countered. He had proved to be a very intense guy. I wasn't sure he would take that kind of criticism well.

That should have been the end of it with Josh. I clearly wasn't interested in getting physical with him. And, though he was a nice guy, he didn't offer the witty stimulation I desperately craved from a partner.

Before I figured out how to gently break up with Josh, he surprised me with a call. Regina and her boyfriend,

Mike, had invited Josh and me to a dinner party they were throwing. Josh and Mike were best friends from childhood, and several of their law school friends were also attending. Loneliness is a powerful motivator, so I decided it was worth one more shot. Regina, Mike, and even Josh himself all claimed that Josh was a fun-loving, humorous guy. I could use this opportunity to finally see Josh relaxed, hanging out with friends with whom he felt comfortable. Maybe he'd loosen up and surprise me, I desperately tried to convince myself.

He showed up that Saturday night with a bouquet of beautiful orange Bird of Paradise flowers. "I know orange is your favorite color." He beamed at me. It wasn't. I assumed he was basing that on the nail polish color he had asked me about weeks earlier.

We drove the mile and a half west to Tenleytown, where Regina and Mike lived in a beautifully decorated one-bedroom apartment and joined the party already in progress—Mike and Regina, two other couples, and Josh and me. Crap. We were at a couples party. As a couple. I immediately knew I had made a terrible mistake.

I grabbed a drink and prepared myself for a long night. As I was pouring my second glass, pretending to be interested as one of the couples bragged about running a 5K together, something amazing happened—a single guy walked in. No girlfriend, fiancée, or wife in tow. He was a friend of Regina's from their hometown in North Carolina and had recently moved to Bethesda. More importantly, his presence meant it was no longer a couples party, and for that I was extremely grateful to him. I was sick of talking to couples about couples activities. I introduced myself and made a point not to mention I was there with Josh.

I had hoped that Josh would be relaxed and easygoing in such a familiar environment, but he seemed more on edge than ever. He wasn't speaking to me but stared at me uncomfortably from across the room. At one point, I caught him taking a picture of me with his phone.

Later, when I noticed him sitting on the couch all alone, I went over to check on him. He sat there looking at me, making me incredibly self-conscious. "Those are nice shoes. Why did you wear those tonight?" he asked, clearly jittery. Seriously? This was fourth date conversation?

I stared at my feet to check out which shoes I happened to be wearing. "Uh, I think they were closest to my door." I didn't bother telling him I had worn my sensible shoes since I was no longer interested in impressing him.

"You have an amazing neck," he continued, staring.

"...Uhhh, thanks?" I was visibly confused and uncomfortable, so I got up and returned to the kitchen, leaving him alone on the couch to stare. I couldn't handle whatever it was he was doing.

As I poured my third drink of the night, Mike pulled me aside. "Josh really likes you. Like, he's crazy about you and he's so nervous about tonight." Tonight? I didn't understand why he would be so nervous about attending a party with me. And then it sank in. This was our fourth date. Josh assumed we'd finally be having sex tonight. Shit.

"Just promise you'll take really good care of him," Mike said casually as he walked away.

What the fuck? Who talks like that? I had really miscalculated the way the night was going to go. My friends only knew Josh as "The Face Licker." His friends were planning our wedding.

Josh was making his way back over to the group, so I

involved myself in conversation with De'Anthony, the single guy. But my distraction didn't work. Josh approached, took my arm, and was pulling me toward the bathroom. I resisted, but he pleaded with me to follow. He said he wanted to talk. I assumed he knew that I was on the verge of breaking up with him and began brainstorming ways to let him down gently.

But before the bathroom door was even closed, I felt something moist moving around the outside of my lips. I pulled my head back and told him to stop. When he asked me why, I waved my arm around. "Because we're standing in Regina's bathroom."

"So?" He came at me, tongue protruding. I dodged his advance.

"It's a bathroom. And literally everyone from the party is two feet away on the other side of that door. I'm not feeling particularly amorous."

He ignored me and tried once more to attack my face, but failed. I opened the door and walked out. "That was weird," I said as I caught De'Anthony's eye.

Josh stayed in the bathroom for a while, and the guests soon began to leave. De'Anthony, or De, as I came to know him, remained, and he, Regina, and I enjoyed some pleasant superficial conversation as Mike retrieved Josh from the bathroom. They disappeared into Mike and Regina's bedroom, and, about ten minutes later, they emerged in a cloud of skunky smoke.

Sadly, even the pot wasn't enough to calm Josh's nerves. He began alternately pacing the apartment and lying motionless on the couch.

"There's no way he can drive home tonight." I stated the obvious as Regina, Mike, De, and I watched Josh pace.

"He needs to stay here." No way in hell was I going to take responsibility for him.

Regina and Mike agreed, and I felt suddenly relieved that I wouldn't have to spend my night fending off Josh's drunken, tongue-filled advances. Though I only lived about a mile away, it was approaching 2 a.m. and the residential streets between our two neighborhoods were deserted. Regina called me a cab as De began saying his goodbyes.

"You live right near Caddie's?" I was confirming what he had told me earlier that night. Caddie's was my pub trivia bar in Bethesda.

"Yeah, like on the same block."

"I'm there every Tuesday night with a group of friends. You should join us." He seemed appropriately excited by the invitation, and we exchanged numbers before he took off.

I said my goodbyes and thanked the hosts for their hospitality, trying not to seem as eager as I really was to get out of there. I opted to wait outside for my cab.

Ten minutes later, I was still waiting. It became increasingly clear that my cab wasn't coming, so I walked over to the main road hoping to hail another. After another five minutes I gave up. I knew that getting a cab in that neighborhood would take forever. All the cabs were downtown waiting for the clubs to let out. And the idea of sticking around and possibly running into Josh spurred me to action. Though Uber was technically operating in DC at that point, I had never heard of it. So, I chose to walk myself home through the darkened neighborhood at 2 a.m., keys clenched between my fingers in case I needed to gouge someone in a hurry—the thought of being assaulted by a stranger less terrifying than the thought of being assaulted by Josh.

The next day I dumped The Face Licker.

My foray into set-ups began and ended that summer, leaving my self-esteem in tatters. After failing to connect with so many different types of men, I began to seriously wonder if I had the ability to attract love at all. I appreciated friends wanting to help me find a relationship, but it was obvious they didn't know what I wanted or needed. And, clearly, neither did I.

WISHFUL THINKING

Dating is exhausting. I had just ended things with The Face Licker and was in desperate need of a vacation. Fortunately, my parents rented a condo almost every year in Ocean City, Maryland, just a three-hour drive from DC.

As a young couple in the '70s, my parents had moved to Baltimore and discovered Ocean City before it had become a vacation destination for people in the Delmarva region. Back then, the town was a modest strip of hotels and shops surrounded by vacant stretches of beach. Today it is a narrow, ten-mile strip sandwiched between the ocean and the bay, packed with hotels, condos, restaurants, mini-golf, and fudge shops. Growing up, though we lived in Connecticut, we would vacation annually in Ocean City as a family.

Some people can't stay at the beach all day, every day, but I come from a long line of beach-folk. Each morning, my parents would rise early and claim a perfect spot on the beach, close to the hotel entrance, near a lifeguard, but beyond the reach of the late afternoon shadows cast by the high rises. They'd then return to the condo to rouse us kids. After we ate breakfast and packed our lunches, my dad would load us up with beach accoutrements and herd us down to our awaiting blankets. I could spend hours in the ocean. I loved diving through the rough surf after a storm or floating atop the gentle waves on calm days. After lunch we'd play Uno or a game of cribbage before diving back into the water; late afternoons passed reading Patricia Cornwell novels until I fell asleep in the sun.

We had all the latest beach technology: a rolling cooler that transformed into a table when closed, a cart with extra-wide wheels for easy rolling over the sand, umbrella anchors with attachable tabletops. Add to that the twine and duct tape my dad, the engineer, carried around in his beach bag for beach-related emergencies. We almost never had to return to our room. We snickered at the novices who fled inside to eat lunch or had to chase their stray umbrellas down the beach on breezy days. We were pros, maximizing every beachable moment.

As adults, it became more difficult for us to coordinate these family getaways. Arranging time away from work was especially difficult for my brother, a surgical resident. Plus, my sister and brother had both married people who preferred more active vacations. While I loved exploring new cities, I was always willing to take my parents up on their offer of a free week at the beach.

That summer, after making a clean break from The Face Licker, I joined my parents at the Plaza Hotel. I was looking forward to a week of relaxation, but mentally prepared myself for several days of intrusive questions about my dating life. My brother, sister, and their spouses were joining us later that week, which would then hopefully distract my parents from my dating disappointments.

But surprisingly, the first day was silent. Not a peep about my biological clock or their fast-approaching deadline for me to get married. The sun set on the second day, and we retreated inside to shower and get ready for dinner, all without my having to explain why I was still alone. I began to relax, let my guard down. Maybe they were as tired of nagging me about being single as I was of being single.

Feeling refreshed after my shower and a day of doing absolutely nothing, I towel-dried my hair, twisted it into a tight bun, and stepped out into our condo kitchenette. My mom was sitting at her iPad, sifting through some files.

"Want to see pictures from our trip?" My parents had taken a vacation to Austria, Hungary, and the Czech Republic earlier that summer. And, while browsing through hundreds of someone else's vacation photos isn't exactly my idea of a good time, my dad was still in the shower, and I had nothing to do till dinner, so I acquiesced.

"...And this is the Bone Church," my mom was explaining around picture 150 or so. "Almost everything in this church is made from real human bones." I had to admit, the pictures were impressive—a giant bone chandelier, skull garlands strung from the ceiling. "There were so many beautiful old churches over there. We visited a new one practically every day," my mom continued. "Did you know that you're supposed to make a wish every time you enter a new church?"

I had never heard that before and began to wonder how many opportunities I had missed to wish for unlimited wealth or chocolate during my trips to Spain and Italy years earlier.

She continued. "So, I spent my trip traveling across

Eastern Europe wishing for you to find a husband." Her words dropped like the bombs that had decimated those countries in decades past.

That would teach me to let my guard down.

SHAME SPIRAL

Done with the set-ups and feeling again like a relationship failure, I immediately jumped back into online dating when I returned to DC. Dustin appeared very attractive in two out of five of his profile pictures, and he attempted, if slightly missed the mark, on humor in his profile. That was enough for me to at least give him a shot. We quickly made plans to meet over boozy milkshakes—my preferred method of alcohol consumption—at Ted's Bulletin, a restaurant with a modern take on an old-school diner, in Capitol Hill.

It was an odd first date to say the least. Dustin was attractive enough—cuter than his worst pictures, not as attractive as his best pictures. I couldn't tell if his disheveled appearance was on purpose or not. With his mussy hair, uneven beard, and droopy eyes, he looked like he had just gotten out of bed.

We spent the first half of the date discussing ghosts, which was apparently becoming my thing. But unlike my conversation with JD the previous year, this time Dustin initiated. He believed that he had been contacted by the ghost of his best friend from childhood who had died years before. His story and, really, any story about ghosts, gave me goosebumps. I then proceeded to tell him about the ghost I believed haunted my parents' house in Connecticut. People at the tables next to ours were giving us odd looks.

Dustin then switched into overly complimentary mode, telling me all the things he liked about the way I looked. As someone who has trouble taking a non-sarcastic compliment, I became immediately uncomfortable. And his compliments were oddly specific. He pointed out a curl in my hair he particularly liked. He told me that he enjoyed how the shirt I wore hinted at a lot of cleavage but didn't put it all out on display. As I sucked down my milkshake, he commented that I looked like a model in an ad for a malt shop. That's when I knew he was just making shit up.

He then described what was going to happen after we left the restaurant—he was going to take my hand, protect me from cars as we crossed the street, and then make out with me before we parted ways. While I like a guy who's forward, the whole scenario was a little off-putting. It felt like he was running through a script. A script that hinged on my having the IQ of a child who just runs out into traffic. Still, I didn't resist when he grabbed my hand or went in for the kiss. It was sloppy and wet, but at least it stayed on my lips and away from the rest of my face. He had marginal potential.

Our second date was a complete disaster. We met up at a bar in Dupont, and he spent half the night complimenting other women on their attire.

"Wow, you're really pulling off that dress," and "Those shoes make your legs look fantastic." It was simultaneously embarrassing and degrading to watch. The women he harassed all gave me sympathetic looks as they hurried away. I assumed it was a move he had learned in one of those books that teaches you how to get dates by acting like a dick.

I decided I was ready to leave and made it clear I didn't care if Dustin came with me or not. But he followed me out of the bar and half apologized, half insulted me. He told me he didn't intend to hit on other women around me, it's just that he thought I was cool enough to want to chat up strangers at the bar.

When playing back the whole Dustin episode in my head, I can't come up with a rational reason for not ending things with him right then and there. Sure, I had been feeling lonely of late, but I thought I still had some self-esteem. Clearly, I was wrong.

After leaving the bar, Dustin and I walked toward the fountain in the center of Dupont Circle and sat next to each other on a bench. I figured we could continue the conversation about why he was being such a douchebag, but he immediately lunged for my face. The make-out wasn't half bad, drier than the previous session, so I let it continue without protest. He wasn't the greatest guy, or even really a truly decent guy, but he was still reasonably attractive. When his hands began their magic journey to my crotch, I pulled away. I wasn't about to give a show to the homeless men who seemed to be inching closer. Also, the circling rats kind of killed the mood. But Dustin was determined. He pulled me back in and slid his hand under my waistband. I grabbed his arm and angrily told him to stop. He did, reluctantly. And, while staring dreamily at my lips, he casually brought up how it was nice that I lived so close to Dupont. It would be way easier for him to just spend the night with me than for him to return to his car which was parked all the way out at Greenbelt, a good forty-five-minute Metro ride away. I checked the time and told him he'd better get going if he was going to make it back to his car before the trains stopped running.

For reasons that still totally elude me (maybe I had a stroke?), I agreed to see Dustin again. We had had one decent date and one terrible date. I figured date number three would be the deciding date. Also, he offered to cook me dinner at his apartment. Before I left work that day, I wrote down his address in my day planner and on a Post-it note on my desk at work. If Dustin murdered me, I wanted the police to know where to find my body. The mere fact that I thought there was a small chance he would kill me should have precluded another date. But I didn't have anything else going on in my life, and if I survived it might be a story worth telling.

Dustin picked me up from the Silver Spring Metro station after work that Friday evening and drove me the twenty minutes to his condo out in the suburbs. I hadn't realized we would be traveling that far from the Metro, my usual escape route.

Upon arrival, he opened a bottle of wine and put the bacon-wrapped chicken in the oven. We weren't drunk enough to have much to say to each other, so we fooled around until the chicken was ready. I was surprised by how much I enjoyed the make-out and light groping, despite having no feelings for him, and I began to think the night might have some potential. Maybe there was a way I could turn it into a friends-with-benefits situation, except for the fact that I really didn't want him as a friend.

After a delicious dinner and our first two glasses of

wine, I helped Dustin clean up. While loading the dishwasher, I asked if he wanted to watch a movie.

"I'd actually like to take a bath with you." He looked at me, completely serious. He went on to further explain that he had wanted to bathe with me since we met. It all felt very *Silence of the Lambs*.

Any girl in her right mind would have demanded he drive her back to the Metro right that second. I had to think. I hadn't been presented with an opportunity that absurd in a very long time. I was leaving DC the next day for Cam's bachelorette party in Newport, Rhode Island, and was lacking in stories with which to regale my friends.

"That could be romantic," I lied. "Go start the tub. I'll be right in." He practically ran to the bathroom while I grabbed my phone.

"Boy am I going to have a story for you tomorrow," I texted Cam and Sarah. "Oh, and if I don't show up tomorrow you can find my body here." I texted Dustin's address. A girl can never be too careful.

I had never bathed with a man before, though on TV it always looked so relaxing and romantic. But with the nozzle digging into my neck and my legs spread and bent awkwardly, I wondered if anyone could enjoy sharing a regular-sized tub with a partner. It seemed unlikely. Dustin had the foresight to bring the wine in with us.

We exited the bath about forty minutes, and two bottles of wine, later. We were drunk and naked, so we climbed into bed. The sex was unremarkable and thankfully quick, because shortly thereafter the room began to spin. I stared hard at the wall and placed a foot on the floor to keep from getting nauseated. As my eyes focused, I realized I was staring at a box on his closet shelf.

Handwritten across the side of the box in black marker was the word "Evidence." *At least everyone knows where to find me*, I thought right before I passed out.

I came to a few hours later. My head was pounding, and I had to pee. I got up to go to the bathroom, but my legs were like rubber. I held onto the wall and guided myself the short stretch down the hall to the toilet. No sooner had I finished peeing than my stomach began to churn. I turned around and knelt just in time. The entire bottle and a half of red wine I had consumed came back up as my body heaved and contorted painfully.

When it was over, I pressed myself against the cool tile floor until my head started to clear. I then grabbed the edge of the sink, pulled myself up, and stared at my glassy-eyed, mussy-haired reflection in the mirror as I rinsed out my mouth, spitting the remnants of what looked like blood down the sink.

I gingerly crawled back into bed, hoping not to wake Dustin, but it was too late. He was awake and feeling frisky. He started to climb on top of me, but with all the remaining energy left in my body I was able to roll him off. "I just threw up," I snapped. "If you touch me, I'm gonna throw up on you." I rolled over and promptly passed out again.

I awoke at 7 a.m. to a hand between my legs. Dustin was determined, I had to give him that. Somehow, despite vomiting what felt like everything I had ever consumed, I was still drunk and I knew that the motions of sex would bring up whatever was still left in my stomach. I told Dustin as much and suggested he just drive me home.

"Well, why don't I just work on you for now, and if you feel better after, we can try again." I knew I wasn't going to feel better after, but I also wasn't about to say no to the offer.

I lay there on my back motionless as he worked between my legs, alternating between my physical highs and lows. It's difficult to achieve orgasm when you're simultaneously trying not to vomit, but it is possible.

Dustin took my ability to finish as a sign that I was good as new, and he climbed back on top of me.

"Nope. Still gonna vomit," I said as I rolled out from under him. I found my pile of clothes and began to dress to the best of my drunken ability.

Dustin and I rode back to the Silver Spring Metro station in complete silence. I had nothing left to say to him, and he was grumpy that I hadn't put out that morning. "I'm gonna get out here," I said as we pulled up at a red light in front of the Dunkin Donuts across from the station. I gave him a peck on the cheek and was out of the car before he could reply. I staggered into the coffee shop and ordered a coffee and an egg croissant sandwich. My head was pounding, my mouth was dry, and the world felt slightly atilt. I wasn't entirely sure I'd make it to the airport that afternoon.

After inhaling my breakfast, I crossed over to the Metro station. But as my luck would have it, the trains were experiencing technical issues and were running on a twenty-minute delay. My throbbing temples couldn't wait that long, so I hopped on the first bus into Bethesda that I could find and caught the train from there. I called the Chinese restaurant near my apartment while in transit and picked up my deliciously greasy second breakfast on my walk home from the Van Ness station. An hour later, I was slumped over on my couch shoveling spicy Szechuan dumplings and sesame chicken into my mouth. I felt instantly better. I managed to shower, finish packing, and get to the airport on time. By the time my plane took off that afternoon, my hangover had subsided from debilitating to merely painful.

Cam and Sarah picked me up from the Providence airport on their drive down from Boston just before 5 p.m. I was elated to see them, though I didn't look it.

"Looks like you had a rough night," Cam observed from the passenger seat as I poured myself into the back of the car. "What was that text about? Also, are you hungry? We're thinking about getting Mexican."

"Yes. Mexican. I need queso." I filled them in on the events of the previous night as I binged on chips and queso and fajitas. They judged me harshly and with humor, making me grateful for the time alone with them before the rest of the party arrived.

By early afternoon the next day, most of the girls had made the trip down from Boston to the house Sarah had rented for us near the beach. Our first event of Cam's bachelorette weekend was a trip to a local winery. The thought made my stomach churn. My head was still pounding from my night with Dustin, so I offered to be the designated driver while the rest of the girls toasted to Cam.

I remained sober the rest of the weekend, keeping drunk girls from running into the street, ensuring the snacks Sarah had thoughtfully packed for the weekend were free-flowing, and taking pictures of Cam passed out mid wardrobe change and texting them to her fiancé, Dan, for posterity.

Dustin texted me, "Hi," once while I was away. The thought of him was viscerally linked to a feeling of nausea. On my flight home, I experienced a moment of clarity. I decided I needed a detox from both drinking and dating.

Part 3

HAUNTED

SHUTDOWN

Sex. Dating. Romance. Whatever category bathing with guys from the internet falls under. Those things clearly weren't working for me. As summer came to a close, I poured myself into extracurricular activities as both entertainment and distraction. I played on two weeknight softball teams, was captain of my Skee-Ball/cornhole team, and continued to attend pub trivia weekly despite Derek's presence. In addition, I had started as a Saturday volunteer at the National Zoo earlier that summer. I barely had enough time to catch up on *The Real Housewives of New Jersey* each week, another activity I gladly prioritized over dating. Staying busy kept me from feeling lonely; it made me feel social and purposeful.

For a few weeks in late summer and early fall, I was on the go and feeling satisfied with the status of my life. And then, on October 1st, 2013, the government shut down. For almost three weeks I had no job and no money with which to participate in my extracurricular activities. I sat at home all day every day, unable to go anywhere because riding the Metro cost money that I didn't have.

The first week of the shutdown, I was productive. I scrubbed my apartment clean, did my laundry, went through my clothes and made piles for Goodwill.

By week two, I was going stir crazy. I hadn't been able to buy groceries since the shutdown began. I subsisted on a ration of two tablespoons of peanut butter and an apple for lunch every day and picked sparingly at a rotisserie chicken I had purchased at the end of September for dinner. The skin was starting to change colors, but it smelled fine. I spent an hour and a half at the gym in my building each day since I had nothing better to do. I had lost five pounds already.

By week three, I couldn't watch the news anymore. I was tired of seeing Ted Cruz and his cronies tell the media that the shutdown was good for America. I had been forced to file for unemployment and spent my days looking for jobs anywhere but DC. I was sick of the government, and sick of pundits complaining about the free vacation they assumed everyone in DC was enjoying. I was down nine pounds since October 1st.

Fortunately, my friends and family were amazing. A couple weeks into the shutdown I received multiple care packages in the mail, allowing me to survive on only one trip to the grocery store. I subsisted on packages full of candies, homemade treats, and expensive whiskey, and was grateful for gifts of books to help me pass the time and accessories I was now too poor to afford. And Caroline, one of my DC friends, made me a week's worth of dinners that I managed to stretch out for ten days of sustenance that kept me going when the last remnants of my probably-expired chicken had been devoured. The generosity of those around me ensured that if I ate sparingly and didn't care about silly things like vitamins and nutrients, I would survive the month.

I jumped back into online dating just so I would have something to do between applying for jobs and writing angry emails to the Speaker of the House. I had never felt more frustrated or angry, and I wasn't doing a great job of hiding it. My trivia and Skee-Ball friends commented that I seemed withdrawn. The shutdown was all anyone in DC was talking about, and I just couldn't bear it anymore. So I stayed quiet. I stopped arguing with people who told me to loosen the purse strings and go out with my friends because I'd surely get paid retroactively. I ignored the people who told me this was the perfect time to take a relaxing vacation; I could just pay it off later. I stopped participating in my life and prayed for something, anything, to change.

And then, as quickly as it had happened, the shutdown was over. Ted Cruz and John Boehner took their bows and shook each other's hands over a job well done, while I was quietly informed that as a government contractor, I would receive no back pay for the time the government was closed. Cam's wedding in Boston was less than a month away, and I had to decline several pre-wedding activities that she had planned for us bridesmaids. No mani/pedi for me, and I would have to do my own makeup for the wedding while the rest of the girls were pampered by a makeup artist. But, at the end of the day, I took solace in the fact that I would still be able to attend. The plane ticket and dress had been purchased before the Republicans had bankrupted me.

I was angry. Everywhere I went, I heard people complaining about how unfair it was that government employees had gotten three weeks of paid vacation. I bit my tongue and began to pick up side jobs to make up for the paychecks I had lost. Unemployment had helped slightly, but even at the max it didn't cover half my usual paycheck each week. People who complain that unemployment benefits remove all incentive for people to work have clearly never tried to live in a major city on $340/week.

I became a Mystery Shopper—someone hired by companies to shop in their stores, complete tasks, and evaluate the experience. The individual shops didn't pay much, but if I was sufficiently determined I could sign up for shops every week all over the DC area. I also enrolled in two research studies at the National Institutes of Health clinical center. The first was a simple single-visit study testing virtual reality telemedicine appointments. Easiest $75 I ever made. I could finally afford groceries again.

The second study was considerably more uncomfortable, but I was compensated accordingly and highly motivated to get paid. The purpose of that study was to test the effectiveness of an experimental new anti-anxiety medication against the current treatment, Xanax, and against a placebo. Since I was a healthy control who did not suffer from anxiety, the study required the researchers to induce anxiety in me...by shocking me at random intervals with electrodes placed on my wrists. Each week over the course of four consecutive weeks, researchers would give me one of the drugs or placebo and then shock me intermittently for thirty minutes to assess my anxiety levels.

I ran through the lengthy consent form with the lead investigator on my first visit. She explained that I couldn't consume caffeine or alcohol for twenty-four hours prior to my "shock days," nor could I have alcohol for seventy-two hours afterward. I also had to promise to use two forms of birth control during the study to prevent pregnancy. I laughed. Not a problem. I had started chatting with a new guy online during the shutdown, but I wasn't terribly excited about him, and my encounter with Dustin over the summer had reminded me that casual sex was usually more trouble than it was worth. He had left me feeling emotionally beat down and physically ill. I had no desire to repeat that experience.

I arranged to begin my part of the study two weeks later. I had Cam's wedding in the interim and didn't want to show up twitching or suffering from other unforeseen side effects.

The shutdown had broken my spirit. Maybe the electrodes would zap me back to life.

TOO GONE, TUCSON

A week later I was in Boston for Cam's wedding. I was finally starting to feel like my old self again—part cynical, part jaded, entirely fun. The shutdown didn't come up once in conversation that whole weekend. It was amazing.

The wedding was held at the Museum of Science, an older building spanning the Charles River where Boston and Cambridge meet. The ceremony took place in a moderately sized meeting room with floor-to-ceiling windows overlooking the Charles River and the Boston skyline beyond. Cam and Dan said their vows as the sun set on the city behind them. It was beautiful. The reception, held on the first floor of the exhibit hall, allowed us to dance the night away among dinosaurs and space shuttles.

And as much as we all wanted to keep the night going, twenty minutes into the after-party, both Sarah and I were done. Having been up since 6 a.m. in beautiful, but uncomfortable formal wear—floor-length royal blue single-strap dresses with boning along the torso—we rushed back to the room we were sharing, eagerly threw on our pajamas, and crawled into bed.

I was just about to turn off the bedside lamp when my phone vibrated. *How's your night going?* It was a text from Chris, the new guy I'd been talking to. I was irrationally annoyed. I hadn't even met this guy and he was texting me at 2 a.m. just to chat. We had made plans to meet that Monday evening, once I was back in DC. But I honestly wasn't looking forward to it and had no interest in late night chatting. I had only responded to his initial OkCupid message out of boredom during the shutdown, and I still wasn't feeling all that hopeful about dating.

I tactfully responded that I was partied out from a friend's wedding and was just about to go to sleep. He didn't get the hint. He tried to keep the conversation going. I finally told him, more harshly than I intended, that the chitchat could wait till Monday and that I wouldn't be responding for the rest of the night. I was asleep by the time my head hit the pillow.

The Monday after Cam and Dan's wedding, Veterans Day, my alarm went off at 7 a.m. Though only a volunteer at the National Zoo, I was required to make up the hours I missed that weekend while away for the wedding. As government employees across the city were still nestled in their cozy beds on that federal holiday, I dragged myself out and headed to the zoo.

I spent my day in the Amazonia exhibit the usual way—cleaning tanks and aquariums, checking water temperatures, preparing diets for the animals, feeding and washing tortoises, and doing general cricket upkeep (cleaning, feeding, and trying my best not to inhale their molted exoskeletons). I left seven hours later feeling physically exhausted and covered in dirt, the mysterious liquid that occasionally dripped from the ceiling, and a small amount of tortoise feces. I would have loved nothing more than to go home and sleep, but I had to prepare for my date with Chris.

After a thorough shower and hair-washing—in case any cricket molts, or worse, live crickets, had gotten stuck—I plopped down onto my bed and did nothing for two blissful hours. At 5 p.m. I forced myself up. I had zero interest in meeting Chris, or honestly anyone, but I told myself I had to get back into the dating world if I didn't want to be alone forever. We were meeting for drinks at Penn Social, a spacious two-story bar downtown that offered large TVs and a projection screen for major sporting events, as well as board games, bar games, and a few video games. I made sure to eat something before I left, since Penn Social was more a bar than a restaurant.

Arriving a few minutes early, I ordered myself a Jameson on the rocks and pulled out the crossword puzzle I had been working on during the train ride over. At 6:30 p.m. on the dot, he strolled in. *Well shit. He's kind of hot.* I immediately wished I had put more effort into my appearance. We greeted each other cheerfully, then he headed to the bar to grab a drink while I did a quick assessment of my appearance. I was wearing a cute-ish outfit—a red peplum shirt with navy blue polka dots paired with a gray cardigan and one of my more flattering pairs of jeans. I pulled my shirt down slightly, which had the simultaneous effect of showing off my cleavage while hiding my love handles. My hair was falling flat, but the curls were tight, and there was nothing I could do about it now anyway. At least I knew it was cricket-free.

Chris returned with his drink, and we began to chat.

He had moved to the DC area the previous month from Pittsburgh to work at a local physics think tank. Though I had lived in DC for years, I still wasn't sure what exactly people did at think tanks. It certainly sounded important though. Conversation flowed naturally with him, and the chemistry was definitely there. The upper bar, where we were sitting, was empty, so we moved downstairs where we had our pick of the bar games. He challenged me to Big Buck Hunter, where I proved to be terrible with a fake rifle. "I'm way better at shooting people," I joked. So he challenged me to a James Bond arcade game where I easily kicked his ass. After next beating him in a few rounds of Skee-Ball, we settled in at the bar for another drink. I was acutely aware of how close he was sitting to me, and of his hand resting firmly on the small of my back.

He was explaining something about his job to me, but most of it was over my head. I was also starting to feel the two Jamesons I had finished. Chris and I were sharing my third.

"So, do you know what xenon is?" I realized Chris was asking me a question.

"You mean the inert gas?" I hoped there wouldn't be any xenon-related follow-up questions.

His smile widened as he praised me for knowing my noble gases. And then he kissed me. If I had been told earlier in life that knowledge of the periodic table would result in attractive men kissing me, I would have paid a lot more attention in chemistry class.

It was chilly when we exited the bar at 9:30 p.m., but my cloak of Jameson kept me warm. "Where should we go next?" he asked, his hand still on my back.

The exhaustion I had felt earlier that day had

disappeared. "How about Iron Horse? It's just a few blocks up." I began leading him up 7th Street. We had only gone a block when Chris grabbed my hand, spun me around, and kissed me up against the window of the Red Velvet Cupcakery. My head was swimming from the whiskey, but I felt amazing.

After a very thorough, appropriately moist kiss, and the realization that there were still people sitting by the cupcakery window against which I was pressed, we disentangled and finished the short trek to Iron Horse. The upstairs bar was deserted, and we sat in the corner and continued to get to know each other in between make-out sessions. He was a great kisser. He never once tried to shove his tongue down my throat, and my face was completely dry when we finished.

I nursed a beer and some water for another hour while we did our best to make the bartender and the occasional patron uncomfortable. Just after 10:30, Chris paid our tab and I began to walk us toward the Metro station when he asked, "Where to now?"

I knew Tuesday morning was going to be rough if I didn't get at least one decent nights' sleep that weekend, but I didn't want the date to end. "Clyde's has a reverse happy hour." I explained that while most bars in the area had happy hour till 7 p.m., Clyde's, a restaurant just up the street, ran a happy hour special from 9 p.m. to midnight.

Before I knew it, we were seated at the upstairs bar at Clyde's, an enormous restaurant with four bars and multiple dining rooms decorated in a lavish Victorian style. We ordered a burger (to split) and more drinks. Chris was charming and funny and ridiculously good-looking. I couldn't take my eyes off his smile. His hand rubbed my back as we talked.

At 11:30 p.m., realizing if we stayed out any later we'd miss the last trains home, we made our way down to the Gallery Place Metro station and made out on the platform until my train arrived. I barely slept that night.

I didn't hear from Chris again for a few days, but he eventually texted to say hi. He mentioned that he would be at his parents' house in New Jersey that weekend, but we made tentative plans to see each other the following week. The next week came, and though we texted a few times about possible plans, he said he was too busy at work. His work apparently extended well into the weekend, and by Sunday I was sure I was never going to see him again. Thanksgiving was that Thursday and he was leaving to visit extended family in Chicago on Tuesday night.

To my surprise, on Tuesday afternoon I got a text from Chris. He asked if I was available to meet downtown. He was able to get out of work an hour early and wanted to see me before his flight that evening. It seemed strange that with all the hours he'd been working he was suddenly able to leave early. But, hey, it was a holiday week. Maybe his bosses were feeling generous. I raced downtown, much too desperately, and met him for happy hour. We talked and laughed and shared holiday plans, and his physical affection put to rest the doubts I'd been having.

He left at 6:30, but texted me till his plane took off. He told me all the right things, and, as usual, I swooned.

I enjoyed a wonderful and uneventful Thanksgiving in Connecticut with my family, returning to DC Saturday afternoon to avoid the chaos of the Sunday-after-Thanksgiving travel. My two roommates were still away, so I had the apartment to myself and was taking full advantage by blasting music while baking several batches of Christmas cookies. I took a break to lick a spatula coated in ganache and noticed a new text message from Chris. He had just gotten back from Chicago and asked if I was free the next morning for brunch. We made plans to meet in Alexandria, Virginia, where he lived, the next morning. I didn't even mind that Alexandria was about an hour, and two Metro lines, away. I was elated, and I spent the rest of my night dancing around my kitchen, singing and eating cookie dough.

The next morning we met at Columbia Firehouse, a converted firehouse that now served as a cozy eatery a few blocks from the Alexandria waterfront. He kissed me hello, and we discussed our respective Thanksgivings while we awaited our food. We shared our meals when they arrived. Then he grabbed a local paper off a nearby shelf, and we leisurely sat and completed the crossword puzzle together, his arm around me the whole time. We were so disgustingly cute I hated myself a little bit.

After brunch, we strolled around the waterfront. A gazebo jutted out into the river, surrounded by moored boats. Chris led me out to the gazebo, where we kissed and made pretend future plans to be rich and own a boat together. He then took my hand in his and walked me through the Torpedo Factory, an old building along the water that was used in the manufacture and maintenance of torpedoes in the early 1900s and now served as coveted space for artists to work and sell their goods. We walked hand in hand through several spaces, taking in the art.

"What's your favorite piece so far?" he asked as we left a small studio filled with metal carvings of animals.

"Sooo, I hate to say it, but I'm not really a huge art

appreciator. I liked a painting in that first room we went in. I think it was of leaves?" I knew so little about art I couldn't even pretend to like it properly.

"Oh thank God," he said, squeezing my hand. "I'm not really into art either. Wanna get out of here?" I nodded and we began walking aimlessly up King Street, the main strip in Alexandria. It was approaching 2 p.m., so I figured he'd walk me back to the Metro and call it a day. "Any interest in a movie? Ooh, or there's this hilarious TV series I think you'll really like. If you don't have any place you need to be, I live just a few blocks up."

As it happened, I didn't have any place to be, so we set off toward his apartment. We ended up binge-watching the first season of *Eastbound & Down*, an absurd HBO comedy about a self-destructive former Major League Baseball player. The show was hilarious, and the experience was enhanced by Chris's arm wrapped around me. Also by the glasses of wine we were pounding.

"You kind of remind me of Danny McBride," Chris joked, referring to the overweight, squinty-eyed main character of the show. "You're really funny, and you've got the same curly hair." He tugged on one of my curls. I hoped that was where he thought the similarities ended.

When the first season concluded a few hours later, Chris scooped me into his arms and kissed me. The show hadn't exactly been an aphrodisiac, but making out with a hot guy certainly was. His hands began to lift my shirt and I quickly acted to stop him. "My clothes will be staying on today." My heavy breathing didn't really underline the seriousness of my message. But I had made a conscious decision not to get too physical with a guy too soon. I had had too many awkward sexual situations with men and wondered if it might be the reason my relationships never progressed. I decided I should at least wait long enough to determine if they were going to ghost or, in the case of Dustin, be a total weirdo who wants to bathe with me. I never wanted to have sex again with someone who was just going to disappear or leave me full of regret.

Still, I hadn't vowed to not have fun. So we fooled around on his couch for almost an hour. Sure, his clothes came off, but I felt accomplished in keeping mine on. The sun was almost down when we disentangled ourselves from one another.

"What do you want to do for dinner? We can go somewhere or order in." It was after 5:30, and the date was still going. He didn't seem concerned with getting rid of me.

I surveyed him in his boxers and suggested we order in so that he didn't have to put on real clothes. I liked him better this way. He was tall and very clearly worked out, based on the number of distinct ab muscles I could count. He called in an order for pizza, and we snuggled up on the couch to begin season two.

I left his place at 10:30 p.m. after pizza, more TV, and another hour of fooling around on his couch. The Metro ride home was a blur as I relived the day over and over in my head. I didn't even care that I hadn't done any of my weekend chores. I had no groceries and my apartment was a mess. I couldn't stop smiling.

Surprisingly, it didn't bother me when I didn't hear from him for a few days. He wasn't the greatest with phone or text communication, but he seemed to eventually surface. When I hadn't heard from him by Thursday, I took the initiative and asked if he was interested in doing something Friday night. I was busy most of the weekend, but I was excited to see him again, though I tried to keep my eagerness out of my text.

Can't tomorrow. Gonna be at work till late. On our date earlier that week, he had told me about his family's annual tradition of spending two weeks in Tucson with family friends at Christmas. Since he had just started his job in October, he hadn't accrued enough vacation days for the trip. He was going to be working nights and weekends until he made up the time. I was disappointed, but I felt worse for him. He said it would likely take him a month of extra hours to cover those two weeks.

I enjoyed my weekend at various holiday parties, telling my close friends about my amazing eleven-hour date. Later the next week I tried again: *Any chance you have a break coming up this weekend? You probably need a beer by now.*

Can't 🙁 *Going back to NJ to see my parents this weekend.*

That was strange. He had previously told me he only saw his parents two to three times a year, and this trip was his second to New Jersey in the month since I met him. But I didn't know him that well. I did my best not to jump to conclusions, even after he informed me that he had limited phone reception in the small town where his parents resided, and therefore wouldn't be able to talk all weekend. My immediate reaction was suspicion, but given how negative I'd been about dating lately, I decided to cut him some slack.

As expected, I didn't hear from him that weekend. The radio silence continued through the week. He had told me early on that because of the sensitive nature of his work, he wasn't allowed to keep his phone on him during the workday; he stored it in a locker each morning and retrieved it when he left. I knew other people, trusted friends, who had similar requirements for their important-sounding jobs, so this didn't strike me as unusual. And, since Chris was working such long hours, I tried to rationalize to myself, he probably wouldn't have access to his phone till late every night when he finally left work. By then, maybe he was just too tired to talk.

Despite my best efforts at denial, I was unable to fully convince myself that Chris was just a super-important entry-level physicist who liked hanging out in the deep woods of New Jersey with his parents on weekends. The familiar sense of dread washed over me. I was leaving for Christmas in Connecticut the next weekend and refused to spend another holiday moping over a ghost. I decided that I wasn't going to let Chris just disappear. If he wanted to stop seeing me, he would have to acknowledge me to do so.

I wanted so badly to be a bitch, to call him out on what I now assumed to be his many lies. But instead, my text came out polite and noncommittal. *Hey, I'm assuming this is over since I haven't heard from you in a while. I get that these things don't always work out, but please respond and let me know for sure.*

His response was equal parts confusing and infuriating. *No no, I still want to see you. I've just been so incredibly busy. I'd love to see you again.* Really? Could have fooled me.

I gave it some time but still responded too quickly. *Are you around at all this week? I leave for CT Saturday.* I was such a simp.

Ahhhh, I wish. I leave for Tucson tomorrow.

I had no idea what to do with that exchange. I hadn't seen him since December 1st, and now he was gone till January. He claimed he still wanted to see me, but I wasn't so sure that was true. I decided that rather than jump to any conclusions, I would just text him in a few days to see how Tucson was. If I never heard back, that would be the end of it. Unless of course his phone didn't work in New Jersey *or* the southwest. In which case I might hear from him in January.

On Wednesday evening, while on the train to Dupont to celebrate a friend's birthday, I sent Chris a casual, *How's Tucson? Relaxed yet?* text. I then tucked my phone back into my purse and joined my friends in the empty front room of One Lounge. The group all asked if I had figured out the "Chris situation." I explained that I hadn't, but that it was likely I'd never hear from him again.

Twenty minutes later, while we were in the middle of a conversation about the purchase and upkeep of synthetic merkins, a group of four—two guys and two girls—was led into the otherwise empty room and seated at the table perpendicular to ours. "Wow, that guy is Chris's doppelganger," I told my friends, pointing to the tall guy in the white collared shirt.

I turned back to my friends to learn more about the assortment of merkins available on Amazon but was soon distracted by just how much the guy to my left looked like Chris. I found myself stealing quick glances at his table, but the guy in the white shirt had his back to me and I could only see his profile.

My friend John, sitting to my right, noticed how distracted I had become. "Does this Chris guy have any distinguishing characteristics?" he asked.

I couldn't think of anything, so John prompted, "Is he right- or left-handed?"

"Oh, umm, left-handed," I replied, remembering our afternoon crossword puzzle session a few weeks before.

"Well, that guy over there is wearing his watch on his right wrist. That generally means he's left-handed." I then pulled up Chris' online profile pictures and had my friends assess. Both Chris and the White Shirt Guy had very large noses, and similar stubble and hair. But I still couldn't see him full on, making it difficult to tell for sure.

By then, everyone at our table had become interested in my potential drama and started plotting ways to get White Shirt Guy's attention. When the birthday cake came out, our entire table broke out into an extra loud version of "Happy Birthday." Everyone from WSG's table turned to look. Though I was watching the birthday girl, I noticed WSG out of the corner of my eye. He assessed our table, then quickly turned away. He repositioned himself awkwardly, sitting at an angle so that I could no longer see his profile, just his back. He then rested his head on his left hand, blocking his face from view in a position that didn't look natural or comfortable. Short of donning a trench coat and fake mustache, this guy was doing what he could not to be recognized. It had to be Chris.

Shortly after, a waiter came by with a plate of calamari that no one at our table had ordered. Though there was only the one other occupied table in the room, the waiter loudly addressed the room: "Did someone order calamari?" Again, everyone at WSG's table turned to look. Everyone except him. He kept his back to me, his head obscured by his hand for the rest of the evening. It was amazing how committed he was to not acknowledging me. I've been dumped or ghosted by a lot of guys in my time, but this by far was the most effort a guy had gone through to completely ignore me. It was almost touching.

Sadly, it was in that moment that I realized that I would never have what it takes to be a reality TV star. It was the perfect setting for confrontation—a near empty bar with a ton of my friends on hand just in case I needed backup. But I couldn't bring myself to approach him. I didn't have any snappy one-liners or perfect insults at the ready. I hadn't done any hand-strengthening exercises to enhance my hair-pulling skills. Financially, I wasn't ready to incur the costs associated with flipping the table and breaking all the dishes. I was a disappointment. And I just had questions. *Why had he gone through the trouble of telling me he wanted to see me and then lying to me about being away when I had already given him an out? Was he in a relationship with someone? Or was he just an asshole?*

WSG was clearly spooked after the calamari incident. Though his group had only just received their food, he asked the waiter to pack it all up, and they fled the bar with their barely-touched entrees. But as he was leaving, he made his mistake. He turned and looked right at me. It was Chris. I deleted him from my phone immediately and felt a small sense of satisfaction that at least I hadn't slept with him.

Among my group of friends, "Tucson" is now synonymous with the mythical place people go to disappear. As in, "I can't believe you haven't heard from him. You think he's in Tucson?" Tucson must be a seriously amazing place, where attractive and charismatic people converge to share tales of their latest exploits and serve as alibis for one another. Though I hear the cell reception's terrible.

PLA*TOE*NIC

You can't have too many friends. A few weeks before the government shutdown, I had reached out to De'Anthony, the single guy from the uncomfortable dinner party with The Face Licker earlier that summer. He lived in Bethesda and had said he was interested in joining me for trivia sometime. Since that's how I had met so many of my past and present friends in DC and elsewhere, I decided to pay it forward in the hopes that he could make some friends and maybe become a regular in our group.

He accepted my invitation and showed up one Tuesday evening in early fall freshly showered, nicely dressed, and wearing a subtle, but delightful cologne. "How's Josh?" He smiled as he asked the question. It had been pretty obvious to him at that couples party that I would not be dating Josh much longer. "Are you guys still together?" Since De and Josh were both friends of Regina, I very diplomatically explained that the chemistry just wasn't there. I didn't mention his face-licking tendencies.

"You know that guy's interested in you, right?" My friends teased me about De later that week. I adamantly denied it. I honestly hadn't gotten that vibe from him.

The following Thursday De asked if I wanted to grab a drink after work. I countered with Friday, since I had Skee-Ball and cornhole on Thursdays. He was going out of town that Friday for a long weekend, but we made plans to grab drinks when he returned the following week. My friends continued to tease me, but I insisted that he was just a friendly guy. This guy didn't seem weird or douchey enough to be interested in me anyway.

But that Saturday the texts started rolling in. De sent several pictures of Atlantic City, where he was vacationing with friends. The tone was still friendly, and I found myself wishing I was back at the beach with Cam and Sarah.

But somehow, in the short time between Saturday and Monday night, the tone became flirtatious. He told me he wished I was with him, enjoying the sunset over the horizon, and that he couldn't wait to get back to DC to see me. I didn't know how to respond. Don't get me wrong, I enjoyed the flattering male attention, especially since I had been removed from it for several weeks, but physically De wasn't my type at all. He had a lean, sinewy body and the lanky limbs of a basketball player. He was never going to be able to pick me up and hold me against a wall or throw me onto a bed. Still, I liked him enough as a person to see where this flirtation went. I also appreciated his directness, though that was likely due to the large amounts of alcohol he was consuming with his buddies.

He spent the week texting me, reiterating how much he was looking forward to seeing me. By the time Friday afternoon rolled around, I had let my expectations get the better of me.

We met on the outdoor patio at the Daily Grill in Bethesda. No sooner had I sat down next to him, my skirt intentionally riding partway up my thigh, than he informed me that he had a friend coming into town that evening and had to leave in an hour. We rushed through small talk, discussing how long we'd each lived in the area, where we were from, how many siblings we had, and forty-five minutes later he was paying our tab.

At the top of the Metro station stairs, he pulled me in for a tight hug and told me he had a great time. Then he was off down the street to meet his friend. I descended the steep Bethesda Metro escalator, running through our prior conversations and the evening in my head. I decided that I had misread the entire situation, and he must have just been super drunk when he sent those texts. He probably hadn't meant for them to be flirtatious.

After that, De and I continued to talk via text and Gchat, though the few attempts we made to get together always fell through, and the government shutdown had made me bitter. Our relationship hadn't again encroached on romantic; it felt entirely platonic. But, the day after Chris fled to Tucson, De Gchatted me and I unloaded about what had happened. De was just the ear I needed, and, over the course of an hour, the conversation slowly crept back into flirtatious territory.

Though I wasn't emotionally distraught over the Chris fiasco—I had only gone on three dates with the guy over the course of a month and a half—I felt disappointment over another failed relationship attempt and anger at being lied to. I eagerly accepted De's attention.

"So what's your fetish?" De eventually asked me. "Everyone's got something."

"You mean what am I secretly into? Or what type of fetishist would be into me based on what I'm willing to do?" I asked. I had no intention of answering either of those questions honestly.

"Both," he replied.

As I thought about how to respond, I bit at my thumbnail. "Toe-thumbs," I typed. I then continued that as a child I had been in a freak ice-skating accident and that the doctors had replaced my thumbs with my big toes. "I have thoes! Some guys are REALLY into that. And it's convenient because the reattachment surgery resulted in heightened sensation, and now I love having my thoes sucked." Sure, it was a lie for me, but I bet someone out there was into it.

"You're not serious, right?!" And a minute later, "But, I mean, have you ever tried it?"

We joked around some more, but I eventually admitted that I had never had my thoes, or any of my digits, sucked in a sexual or romantic way.

"Do you wanna try it?" he asked casually, as if he had asked if I wanted to go see a movie.

Though a little grossed out at the general thought of someone sucking on toes, I told him I'd think about it, knowing that he and I rarely followed up on the activities we planned. I intended to ignore the proposition the next day, to let the idea die. But that day at work I got an unusual surprise. One of the women I worked with had gotten me an early Christmas present. I unwrapped the many, tiny tissue paper–wrapped items one by one: cuticle oil, expensive soap, foot scrub, foot lotion, a combination pumice stone/foot brush/emery board, and moisturizing foot socks.

"You are not going to guess what I just got," I immediately Gchatted De, explaining the foot care–related gifts. "It's a sign. I'm in." We made plans to get together after the holidays and I went home that evening and began sampling my presents.

I traveled to Connecticut for Christmas—a far better Christmas than the previous year, despite all that had happened with Chris. I was able to get together with several of my hometown friends, and then traveled up to Boston a few days later to surround myself with more close pals. I have always felt grateful for my friends, and the time with them was exactly what I needed to recharge. We laughed at my ability to drive men to Tucson, pondered whether toe-sucking would be enjoyable or just plain weird, cooed over their young children, ate far too much junk food, and danced the nights away.

While getting ready to go out one night in Boston with Cam and Sarah, I got a Facebook message from a trivia friend. He had just run into Derek on the street. Astonishingly, Derek had been holding hands with a girl. An actual human girl. Apparently, socially awkward Derek had overcome his aversion to physical contact and had gotten himself a girlfriend.

I immediately felt sick. Not because I was still interested in Derek—I wasn't—but because I remembered how careful Derek had been to avoid physical contact with me; how he had used very flimsy excuses not once, but twice, to avoid the possibility of making out with me. I had hoped for my sake that he was just asexual. Turns out he just wasn't into me. At all. That night, with my ego completely deflated, I did what I did best: I went out with Cam and Sarah, danced my way over to the most attractive guy I could find on the dance floor, and made out with him. It wasn't a lasting solution, but it certainly helped.

I wasn't looking forward to returning to DC where I could run into Derek and his new girlfriend at any moment. Nor was I looking forward to New Year's Eve, which in general was a night of far too much build up and far too little delivery. Fortunately, New Year's Eve flew by uneventfully, and before I knew it, it was 2014. I could only imagine the exciting new ways guys would disappoint me this year. So many possibilities!

With no dating options on the horizon and little motivation, I met up with De that first weekend in January. I was nervous for a variety of reasons. First, De and I barely knew each other, and though we occasionally flirted, we had never actually done anything more than hug. Though physically De wasn't really my type, I assumed, and hoped, that the toe-sucking would be a prelude to more inappropriate touching. It had been a while. Second, I was concerned that I might really hate the toe-sucking and end up disappointing him. Third, I was concerned that I might really enjoy the toe-sucking, in which case, would I have to start trolling the internet for serious fetishists?

When I walked into De's studio apartment that Sunday afternoon, he was watching football. He welcomed me with a hug, then sat down on his couch and made no effort to turn the game off, so I joined him. The lights were dimmed and he had lit a candle, but the general vibe was wholly unromantic. Then again, I wasn't sure toe-sucking was a romantic venture. I had never felt so uncomfortable with a guy in my life. I was sweating.

We exchanged pleasantries and spoke about our holidays, and he showed me all the basketball-related gifts he had received from his family. I feigned interest in his new Nike Jordans and training shorts, but secretly thought about how pissed I'd be if those had been my gifts. Then, abruptly, I heard, "So, let me see what I'm working with." He motioned toward my feet.

Unsure of how to unveil my freshly scrubbed, lotioned, and polished toes, I removed my shoes and placed my feet in De's lap. He rubbed them briefly, then with no warning or fanfare, my toes were in his mouth. For just over five minutes he licked and sucked my toes one by one, all with the football game going in the background. I had no idea where I was supposed to look or if I was supposed to help out in some way, so I just watched the game. I can't quite describe the feeling of having my toes sucked—while slightly relaxing, it was mostly just warm, though not altogether unpleasant. And then, as abruptly as it had begun, it was over. My toes were suddenly wet and cold, and De was eyeing the game.

I left my feet on his lap, assuming the physical contact had only just begun, that the toe-sucking had been foreplay. But when he got up to grab a glass of water, I realized that I had shaved my legs for nothing. Was toe-sucking on its own now an acceptable pastime?

We spent another hour watching the game and chatting. It was great getting to know him a little better, but I left his apartment feeling more than a little disappointed. And very much in need of a shower.

SNOW JOB

I was still half-heartedly doing the online dating thing, logging in to delete the messages from the usual milieu of guys posing in shirtless selfies in their bathroom mirrors and messages that read, *Sup?* and *I like ur pics. Wanna meet?* I was on autopilot, deleting away, when I noticed that a guy named Neal had written a grammatically correct, humorous message. I immediately checked out his pictures. He wasn't startlingly attractive in his photos, but he wasn't shirtless or in his bathroom in any of them either. And his profile and messages were genuinely playful and seemed sincere. We quickly set up a date, and in mid-January I met him at a bar in Georgetown for drinks.

I arrived early and strategically placed myself in a seat facing the door so I could eye the patrons entering and leaving. After a few minutes, he walked in. *Damn*, I thought. *Not attractive.* For the most part, he was average-looking—average height, average build. But there was something about his face. It wasn't chubby, exactly, it just seemed slack, with no distinction between his neck and his chin. I lowered my expectations accordingly and waved him over. *God, I hope he's funny*, I wished as I ordered a vodka soda. And, after an initial awkward introduction, he showed me that he was. In fact, he was pretty damn hilarious. And, even better, when he smiled, his whole face transformed. He was reasonably attractive, as long as I kept him smiling.

I found out that Neal had been in the Army, stationed in South Korea. Upon his return to the US, he joined the reserves and worked as a warrant officer, a job I didn't quite understand, but I knew he was required to wear his uniform every day. I didn't even know if I liked him, but I hoped I'd get to see him in uniform one day. For all the banter, we didn't really have much in common—he hadn't gone to college, he was an avid skier, he was born in Canada and raised in California, and he lived in suburbs of Virginia, well beyond the reach of the Metro trains. Still, aside from being funny and increasingly attractive, in part due to the smiling and in part due to vodka, he proved to be physically affectionate and reliable. He texted me almost daily, often just to say hi or send me a humorous meme or gif.

I liked him enough, but I wasn't swooning, which thankfully made me act much more clear-headed than I normally did around men I was dating. On our third date, he mentioned a ski trip he was taking with his friends the upcoming weekend and invited me to join. It was a spur of the moment invitation that I'm not entirely sure he meant to extend, and I was quick to decline. It was way too soon to be hanging out with him and his friends for the weekend, and I just knew that if I accepted the invitation, it would make me appear clingy or needy or whatever it is guys tell themselves to rationalize ghosting.

For our fourth date, I invited Neal over to watch the opening ceremony of the Sochi Olympics. Given the terrible press Sochi had been receiving in the days leading up to the torch lighting—athletes locked in bathrooms, wild dogs roaming hotels, water unfit to drink or use on the skin—I was hoping for a major prime-time blunder. But, far from that, the opening ceremony was incredibly dull. After watching actors dressed as bears and trees float in over the crowd, we quickly lost interest.

We made out for a bit out of boredom, and I discovered that he oddly used almost no tongue when kissing. Every now and then I found the tip of his tongue, but it always retreated when discovered. *Still*, I found myself thinking, *it beats the hell out of too much tongue*. I thought of The Face Licker and instinctively wiped my mouth.

We hadn't yet turned off the ceremony, and Imperial soldiers filled the screen. "Imperialism really turns me on," I whispered as Neal's hands found my breasts. "Now make like Putin and take off your shirt." He laughed and acquiesced.

We fooled around for a bit, but to his disappointment, I managed to keep all but my shirt on throughout the date. Unlike most of the Olympians using Tinder at the Olympic Village that night, Neal wasn't getting any. I remembered how thankful I was that I hadn't slept with Chris, and I congratulated myself after Neal left. I was making him work for it, and so far he seemed more than willing.

Though we had been on four dates and he made no signs of retreating, I still didn't trust that he liked me as much as he intimated. Nor was I sure that I liked him as much as I should for someone I was speaking to regularly.

I hadn't even told my friends about him. They knew I had started seeing someone, but I refused to provide details since I was still well within the ghosting timeframe. Still, he was decent enough that I was willing to take the two Metro trains to a bus out to suburban Virginia for date number five. If that's not a vote of confidence, I don't know what is.

It took me almost an hour and a half to get from my office to the bar he chose in the Shirlington, VA, but I didn't mind. I was looking forward to seeing him, as his texts had become more thoughtful and sweeter in the week after our Olympics date. As we ate pub food and tried our hand at darts, heavy snow began to fall, blanketing the sidewalks and streets. The news was calling for heavy accumulation (which in DC meant anything over two inches) and it was expected that the government would close the following day.

Neal asked me back to his place to watch a movie, but I knew I had a long trek back home and the roads would be treacherous for the Metro buses. I checked my phone to make sure the buses were still running and to look up the schedule for my return trip.

"Just stay over tonight," he offered when he saw me looking at bus schedules. "Work's gonna be canceled. We can sleep in and I'll drive you home in the morning." I considered his suggestion carefully, and in the end, I decided I'd much rather get a ride home in his all-terrain vehicle than chance a ride home on a bus and two trains before the roads could be plowed and the sidewalks shoveled.

We retreated to his place and curled up, watching the always seductive movie *Blades of Glory* followed by several episodes of the cartoon *Archer*. I knew he was expecting sex, but I wasn't yet willing to make the leap of faith that he'd be sticking around. Still, I threw him a blow job to let him know that sex would be on the table in the near future. If we had a near future.

As we were lying in bed, Neal mentioned that he would be out of town the upcoming weekend on a ski trip. I felt a bit of disappointment for two reasons: 1) I was starting to like him and wanted to see him again soon, and 2) Friday was Valentine's Day. I had no expectations of him for Valentine's Day; after all, we weren't exclusively dating. But still, a small part of me hoped he'd want to at least grab a drink and give me another chance to decline sex.

As I silently moped in his arms, he continued. The weekend following Valentine's Day he was planning yet another ski trip with his buddies. That meant that he'd be out of town for two weekends in a row. I felt uneasy. I wondered if skiing was his version of going to Tucson. *Was he just laying the groundwork early so he could phase me out in the coming weeks?*

I was lost in my suspicious thoughts when he surprised me. "Would you be interested in joining us?" he asked. It took a moment for me to realize that he was inviting me along on a weekend trip with his friends. Unlike the previous invitation, which had felt like an accidental invite, this felt intentional. I was surprised that he was extending another invitation to go skiing so soon. I don't ski, but I immediately responded that I'd love to join him. He must have genuinely wanted me to come if he bothered to keep asking. As I drifted off to sleep next to Neal that night, I allowed myself some brief moments of joy, before chastising myself for getting excited about something that would probably never happen.

Work was canceled the next day, as expected, and the morning brought the usual awkwardness of two people waking up together for the first time. I wasn't sure if he was a morning person, so I kept my distance physically—not trying to cuddle or kiss him unless he initiated, which he didn't. After getting dressed in silence, we chatted about the weather and trekked through the snow to grab coffee and muffins at the only open coffee shop in the town center.

He drove me home through the semi-plowed streets in his Jeep. With no cars on the road and snow decorating the cityscape, the drive should have been peaceful. But in the light of day, without alcohol to encourage us, it seemed Neal and I had very little to say to each other. I began to wonder if I should have declined the ski invitation. It didn't feel like we were ready for anything that could be misinterpreted as a step toward a relationship. But, though the ride was awkward, the kiss goodbye was warm and deep. Well, as deep as a kiss can be with a guy who doesn't use tongue.

The next day was Valentine's Day. I had plans to meet Kat downtown for a chocolate and wine pairing event, followed by dinner with her and Angela, who was taking the bus down from New York for the weekend. Though Neal and I had been texting daily, I decided that morning to avoid contacting him that day so as not to give off a desperate-for-a-Valentine vibe. But again, he surprised me. That afternoon, as he was packing up to leave for his ski trip, he texted me a Valentine's Day gif along with a message telling me how he wished he hadn't already committed to the trip so that he could spend the whole weekend with me. It was as close as I had come to having a Valentine in years. I spent the evening secretly excited while downplaying Neal, still just a nameless online guy to my friends. *Happiness is only temporary*, I rationalized. I figured I'd be lonely again soon enough. No point in celebrating too much. Hubris was a bitch.

The next evening, I attended my trivia friend Maggie's birthday party. With Angela in tow, I met Maggie and some mutual friends for dinner in Bethesda before heading to a bowling alley a few blocks away. While we were waiting for our food, Maggie asked me about Neal. I had been cagey about him in the three-plus weeks we had been dating, and while this would have been the perfect time to fill my friends in about our relationship, I hesitated.

"He invited me skiing next weekend with some of his friends." I was surprised at how disinterested I sounded.

"That's so exciting!" my female friends crooned in unison. "Sounds like he really likes you."

I thought about that sentence. He was sweet and affectionate, but never had he expressed that he liked or cared about me. I still wasn't entirely convinced that he did.

"Yeah," I responded hesitantly. "I dunno. Maybe."

"But he wants to spend the whole weekend with you. And he's going to introduce you to his friends. That's a big deal." My friends seemed oblivious to my dating past. Guys I dated never stuck around.

"True." I sounded as unconvinced as I suddenly felt. "But a lot can change in a week." The joy I had felt just hours earlier had waned, and the reality of my romantic life set in.

Maggie kindly offered to let me borrow her ski gear in anticipation of my big weekend. I accepted, appreciative of the gesture, but had a feeling I'd never get around to using it.

Since I hadn't heard from Neal that day, I decided to text him as we were leaving dinner to see how his trip was going. He still hadn't responded by the time I had finished bowling two games. *He's off having fun with his friends*, I reminded myself. *He'll respond when he gets around to it.*

The birthday group was making plans to head to a bar in Bethesda. I turned to Angela to see what she wanted to do since she was crashing with me that weekend. She didn't seem to be enjoying herself at Maggie's party; however, she sometimes looked dour even when having a good time. It could be hard to tell if she was having fun or not.

"Well, a friend of mine is having a birthday party downtown at Penn Social. But it might be crowded, and I don't know if it'll be any fun." Typical Angela. She often had fun ideas but couched them in doubt so that if they sucked, we wouldn't be mad at her. But, having been friends with her for almost a decade, I could tell she wanted to check out the party downtown. So, I said goodbye to my friends, and we began the very long journey into the city.

Metro was conducting track work on the Red Line that (and every) weekend. So, one hour, and a train, a bus, several new bus friends, and a mile walk later, we arrived at our destination in Chinatown. As annoying as the ride had been, I was looking forward to a little dancing and schmoozing with strangers. The bus-folk had energized me. But, as we waited in line outside the bar for the bouncer to let us in, Angela had a change of heart.

"It looks crowded in there." She stated the obvious. It was a bar in downtown DC on a Saturday night. "I probably won't even be able to talk to my friends, it's so loud." Another statement of fact. "And they're charging a $10 cover. Totally not worth it."

While not a fan of paying covers to get into mediocre bars, I had ditched my friends and we had just spent the better part of an hour navigating the city to get there. I was more than willing to pay the cover and start dancing.

"What else is good around here?" she asked.

Somehow, I managed not to strangle her, and we ended up at Fado, an Irish pub down the street. A cover band was playing, and the familiar riffs of classic rock songs eased the growing annoyance I was feeling. We spent the rest of the evening reminiscing about our wild grad school days and commiserating over failed relationships. I was glad we had the time to sit and catch up.

I still hadn't heard from Neal when the cab dropped us off at my apartment just after 1 a.m. *I guess that means he's having fun.* I smiled as I thought about the fun we'd have with his friends the following weekend, and then immediately shook the thought from my head. It wasn't worth thinking about because it was never going to happen.

When I still hadn't heard from Neal by Monday evening, well after his weekend trip had ended, I knew I was being ghosted. I texted a joke and asked how his trip had gone, half hoping he'd respond, half assuming he wouldn't. What I got was worse: *Fun. Exhausting.*

What was I supposed to do with that? If he was done with me, the polite thing to do was to tell me. The impolite thing to do was to just not respond. If he was still interested, he should have at least been able to cobble together a full sentence. I was irritated by his confusing response, but still interested enough to give it one last shot. Tuesday night, on my way home from an evening class I was taking on the National Institutes of Health campus, I texted to see if he was free later that week to hang out. The guy, who less than a week ago had invited me away for the weekend and claimed to want to spend more time with me, never responded. I suspect he had other plans. In Tucson.

TRIFECTA

I had liked Neal, though that's all it had been. Like. What I felt after he ghosted wasn't sadness about the guy I lost, but pure misery about being ghosted yet again, this time by a guy I wasn't even sure I had feelings for. Worst of all, I had known from the start that that's how it would end. That seemed to be how all my relationships ended these days.

The next evening on my way home from work, as I was mentally preparing for a night of pouting and drinking alone, I ran into Mark, a guy who lived in my apartment building with whom I had become friendly. He was a great dresser—usually in a well-fitting suit or freshly pressed dress shirt and pants—and was quite attractive despite the slightly milky appearance of his right eye. I exited the elevator onto my floor as he was taking out his trash.

"You're home early," I observed. Usually when I ran into him it was much later. I would be coming back from trivia or Skee-ball and he'd be returning home from the business school classes he attended at night.

"Spring break," he replied, smiling. "I don't have class all week."

I congratulated him on his newfound free time and began walking toward my apartment.

"Hey, wanna grab that drink we've been talking about forever?" Though I hadn't showered or bothered to apply makeup that day, I welcomed a distraction.

We ended up at an Italian restaurant just down the street. As was usual for late February in DC, the weather was gray and cold and damp, so the place was empty. We cozied up at the bar and I found the conversation surprisingly easy.

"...And that's why I'm not gonna get in a relationship again 'til after I finish school." He was finishing a story about the last girl he hooked up with who had turned into a girlfriend and inevitably required more attention than he was able to give at the moment. Clearly, he felt comfortable enough with me to share his romantic history, so I unloaded on him about Neal.

"Yeah, I hate to say it, but guys are just dicks sometimes. No offense, but that guy was clearly just keeping his options open." His assessment of Neal was spot on. We clinked our near-empty glasses and drank to assholes everywhere.

Though I hadn't asked my neighbor about his eye, he must have been used to addressing the topic. Without prompting, he explained that he suffered from sickle cell disease, a blood disorder. As one manifestation of his disease, his retina detached years ago. To correct the problem, he underwent surgery, which had unfortunately been botched, leaving him blind in his right eye. I expressed my condolences as we finished our drinks, then walked the three blocks back to our respective apartments. The dismal evening had given way to a snow/sleet mixture that seemed to twinkle in the streetlights. Tomorrow it would be a gray, sludgy mess, but tonight it was beautiful.

I was unsure if our encounter had been a date or not. Mark had been very clear that he was still open to casual relationships, just nothing serious. Regardless, the pleasant evening had made me hopeful. After a warm shower, I pulled on a comfortable sweatshirt and sweatpants, got into bed, and logged into my OkCupid account to read my messages for the day. While dating Neal, I had still been chatting with other guys online, keeping *my* options open for the inevitable ghosting. So, the next day, when a guy I had been speaking to for about a week asked me out on a date, I quickly accepted.

"There's just one thing you should know," he messaged me. "I have cerebral palsy and I walk with crutches. I completely understand if you want to cancel. I'm used to it."

Wait, what? I opened his profile and began searching for any mention of his condition or pictures with crutches I clearly must have overlooked. Only there were none. I felt misled, but if I rejected him now, I was just a heartless bitch who wouldn't give the guy with cerebral palsy a chance. So, two days later, I nervously awaited his arrival at a bar in Dupont.

I chose a table near the door on the ground floor, so he wouldn't have to maneuver his crutches in the crowded room and up the narrow stairs. *Maybe he's going to be amazing*, I thought, trying to psych myself up. His pictures *had* been attractive, and, though not hilarious, there had been hints at humor in his messages.

As he ambled in the door and slowly approached me, I felt my bubble of hope deflate. He looked nothing like his pictures. He was short and thin and extremely pale—almost translucent. I'm not sure if he had a nice smile because I never saw it. And, as we engaged in conversation, I realized he also wasn't funny. He had recently undergone surgery to remove a thyroid tumor, and had absolutely no issue describing the whole terrible ordeal to me or showing me his scar—his version of *So, where are you from?* He made no attempt to be charming or interesting.

After downing two drinks in just over an hour, I explained that I had to get going. I held the doors open for him and we stepped into the cold. The wind was whipping around us and right through my winter coat.

"Can I walk you to the train?" he kindly asked.

"Don't you need to catch the Blue Line?" He had told me all the tedious details about his commute to and from work once he had concluded his riveting cancer treatment discussion, though I hadn't asked.

"Yeah, but I can take the Red Line to Metro Center and switch there." His downcast eyes and doleful expression told me he knew the date hadn't gone well. He was hoping for one last play—maybe another health condition he hadn't yet told me about because it was prime second date material.

Shit. I was freezing. I could make the walk to the Metro, just one and a half blocks away, in no time. Walking with him, it would likely take ten minutes. That would be ten minutes of bad conversation and freezing my ass off.

"Thanks, but it's right there and we'd be going in separate directions anyway. Doesn't make sense for you to go so far out of your way," I responded diplomatically. We shared an uncomfortable hug, and then I turned and hightailed it to the train. I felt like a terrible person. But at least three minutes later, I was a warm, terrible person.

The next day, when De Gchatted me to hang out and give the toes another try, I decided to continue my week of unexpected dates. I arrived at his studio apartment later that evening, toes primped and preened. This time, rather than sit around watching football, De suggested we put on a movie. Since neither of us could come up with an appropriate movie to set the toe-sucking mood, we settled on *Airplane* and got comfortable on his bed, located against a wall just a few feet behind his couch in his studio apartment. About thirty minutes into the movie and thirty minutes of us sitting awkwardly motionless beside each other on his bed, De suggested I lay on my stomach facing the TV so he could sit behind me and get to work.

I acquiesced. But again, the experience, though soothing, was not sexually gratifying. And, after about ten minutes, he was done, lying next to me watching the movie. When the movie ended we hugged goodbye, and I was on my way home to shower.

De had made no further effort to touch me, no attempt to kiss me. Though given where his mouth had been, I was entirely ok with that.

SECURITY

My dating approach clearly needed to be re-evaluated. The month following my dating trifecta, I couldn't bring myself to sign into OkCupid. I was stuck in an exhausting cycle of dating people I had no interest in or no future with. I threw myself back into my extracurricular activities: Skee-Ball and cornhole games, volunteering at the zoo, the program evaluation course I was taking at NIH on Tuesday nights. I kept busy and decided I was once again done with dating for a while.

My extracurriculars kept me sufficiently occupied, and a few weeks in I realized I didn't even miss dating. I was taking singledom in stride, and, in mid-March, I finally logged back into OkCupid with the sole purpose of disabling my account. Before doing so, though, I felt the need to satisfy my curiosity. Maybe, just maybe, some amazing guy had appeared in the queue during my weeks-long hiatus. I did a quick search for guys nearby with the word "funny" in their profile and began skimming pictures of the usual suspects. I was about to give up on the familiar parade of weirdos when a new picture caught my eye. The thumbnail was too small to really determine if he was attractive, but I knew I hadn't come across his profile before. I clicked on his username and began reading.

This guy was seriously funny. No, not just funny. Witty. And, once I enlarged his pictures, I gleefully realized he was attractive to boot. When he listed *Mystery Science Theater* under his movie preferences, I knew I had my in. Before I could remember that I had logged in so that I could swear off dating for good, I had messaged this new stranger asking if he'd ever heard of Rifftrax.

We spent the next week eagerly messaging back and forth. I should have chastised myself for getting involved with another guy who was likely just going to vanish, but I was too excited to care. I was enjoying the best part of a relationship, the part where we're both really into each other because we know almost nothing about one another.

Jedediah, or Jed, as I soon came to know him, was wittier and more intelligent than any guy I had dated. Once we exchanged numbers, he inundated my phone with messages that consistently made me laugh, and he seemed as eager as I was to meet.

I suggested Penn Social for our first date. The bar had become a first date crutch for me, providing plenty of bar games and activities in case it turned out I had nothing to say to my date. Jed countered with a less ordinary date.

How do you feel about getting into a car with a stranger? he asked.

I had survived a car ride with a man from the internet before, but still, I knew the correct answer, the one my mom and police officers everywhere would tout. *Depends. Are you susceptible to mace?* I asked instead.

The spray or the spiked ball on a chain? Either way, yes. I knew immediately I would go wherever he asked me to, even if I ended up on the news.

We made plans for Sunday evening. In the meantime, as had become standard when I knew I would be getting into a car with a stranger, I wrote down our planned destination in several locations and made sure friends knew to call the cops if I didn't check in with them by midnight Sunday. I then made a list of everything I knew about my date (name: Jed; Employment history: had been in the army for several years and was currently in grad school; age: twenty-nine; likes: funny movies, me [hopefully]) and placed this very helpful list on my bed to give the cops something to go on if my body was discovered in a shallow grave later that week. I placed my pepper spray in my coat pocket but decided a knife would be overkill. Instead, I tucked a pair of scissors in my purse next to my wallet and headed downstairs.

Jed was waiting for me outside my building. Right on time. Though it was late March, it had been snowing most of the day. We greeted each other with relieved smiles, thankful we each looked like our profile pictures, and he sweetly held his umbrella overhead to keep me dry while he walked me to his car.

We drove the forty-five minutes out to Loudoun, Virginia to the Alamo Drafthouse, a theater/restaurant that was showing *The Grand Budapest Hotel.* Our conversation was the usual slightly awkward conversation of first dates, but it came easily, and, with the snow falling, the drive was beautiful. Twenty minutes into the car ride, I loosened my grip on the scissors hidden in my purse. I was pretty sure he didn't intend to kill me. At least not till later.

The food was much more upscale than I would have imagined from a movie theater, and the movie was a typical Wes Anderson comedy: The characters were each quirkier than the last, and the plot was absurd. Jed and I laughed throughout, but as we sat in the car heading back toward the city, I realized I hadn't really had much time to get to know him. As if reading my mind, he asked if I had any interest in grabbing dessert. Murderer or not, the answer to that is always yes.

We ended up at a small restaurant in Dupont Circle, Al Tiramisu, sharing the restaurant's namesake at the bar. The tiramisu was delicious, the conversation even better. As I devoured the remainder of Jed's portion (at his urging), I knew I didn't want the date to be over.

The snow had stopped by the time we left the restaurant, and I braced myself against the blustery air as I began to walk toward his car. "Do you like games?" Jed was several steps behind me, pointing across the street at a hole-in-the-wall called Thomas Foolery.

I wasn't sure what he was getting at, but since I do enjoy games I nodded. "This place is a divier version of Board Room. Do you have time for a quick game?" He was smiling. He had a great smile.

Board Room was a bar just up the street where you could drink and play board games with friends for a small fee. It was usually packed, and at peak times it could be difficult to claim a seat or a decent game. Thomas Foolery was empty except for two people in a corner playing Battleship and a very disinterested cashier/bartender. Jed ordered us each a beer and asked the cashier for Connect Four. I grinned widely as I thanked her for my drink. She just stared at me, clearly annoyed by my cheerfulness.

I lost about fifteen games of Connect Four that night. (Is there such a thing as a Connect Four savant?) But it didn't matter. I was having a great time. And, for the first time that evening, Jed and I were seated across from each other rather than side by side. I found myself studying him during his turns, examining his hazel eyes, his perfectly shorn dark beard, the precise way he held the Connect Four pieces between his long fingers. He was thin, a little taller than average, and his style was casual—a sweater worn over a button-down shirt and loose-fitting jeans. His overall look was neat and attractive. And there was something extremely inviting about his large eyes and slightly crooked smile. I felt comfortable with him. And more than that, I was seriously attracted to him.

Once our glasses were drained, Jed excused himself to use the bathroom. I checked my phone for the time. 11:15. I sent a quick text to my friends to make sure they knew I was ok: *Date going well. Still out. Still alive.*

Jed returned to the table, two hula hoops in hand. He held one out to me with a smile, and I eagerly accepted. There, in the near-empty bar, we held our very own hula hoop contest, hips swiveling wildly in an attempt to keep our hula hoops aloft. I'm not sure how his tiny hips bested my much curvier midsection, but after three consecutive losses, I declared him the victor and applauded him on his gyrating skills. I hoped to see if they translated to other, more exciting activities in the future.

We pulled up in front of my building just before midnight and each told the other how much fun we had. I started to open the passenger door but changed my mind. Instead, I turned to Jed and went in for a kiss. Thankfully, he reciprocated with an entirely appropriate amount of tongue. I was sold. He was attractive, funny, fantastic company, and a great kisser. Damn, it was gonna suck when he ghosted.

I smiled to myself as I rode the elevator to my apartment on the ninth floor. I got ready for bed and threw away the little slip of paper I had left for the police before climbing under the covers. I stared up at the ceiling, wired, as my phone vibrated on my nightstand. Jed had texted to reiterate how much fun he had on our date.

We saw each other two more times over the next four days. That weekend I was traveling to Connecticut to meet my new nephew, Max, for the first time. Jed drove me to the train station that Friday morning and picked me up, flowers in hand, when I returned Sunday afternoon. I knew it was dangerous to let myself feel as happy as I did, but I was powerless to resist.

My thirty-second birthday happened to be eleven days after my first date with Jed. I hesitated in telling him about it because I didn't want him to feel pressured to do anything for the occasion. And truthfully, it would be easier for me to have no expectations of him if he didn't know about it. But three days before the big day Jed asked me what my plans were for the week, and I didn't want to lie. I downplayed the whole thing, explaining that I was turning thirty-two. It wasn't a milestone, and no one was making a big deal about it. It was sort of the truth. Cam was flying into town from Boston that Wednesday—the night of my birthday and just four days after her own birthday—for work. She, Kat—whose birthday was the day before mine—and I were meeting up for a group birthday dinner.

"So, does that mean you're free after dinner on Wednesday?" Jed and I were both half naked in his bed. I was laying on top of him, gazing into his giant hazel eyes, which had quickly become one of my favorite features of his. I kissed him to indicate that yes, I was free after dinner on Wednesday, and yes, I wanted to see him.

"You should spend the night. I can make you breakfast in bed Thursday." He was beaming at me. Though we were already on our fourth date, we had only been dating a week, and I hadn't yet spent the night. Since Thursdays were my telework days, I wouldn't have to worry about rushing home, changing into something work appropriate, and commuting all the way out to my office in Maryland. As long as he had me home by nine on Thursday morning, I was up for anything.

"Sounds perfect," I whispered in his ear and moved my lips down to kiss his neck.

The next day he sent me a text asking how I take my coffee. *Ooh, I like it iced. With skim milk and sugar and served by an attractive shirtless man. At least, that's how I get it at Dunkin Donuts,* I joked. I knew Jed didn't drink coffee, but in the week I had known him he had proven to be incredibly thoughtful. I assumed he was at the grocery store buying all my favorite coffee fixins for my birthday breakfast. I wasn't used to dating guys who were sweet or attentive. I wasn't entirely sure any of the guys I had previously dated even thought about me when I wasn't around. This was refreshing new territory for me.

When my birthday finally rolled around that Wednesday, the workday seemed to last forever. I kept staring at the clock on my computer, hoping it would fast forward to 5 p.m. It didn't help that in the afternoon, done with his grad school classes for the day, Jed was texting me about our evening together.

I'm thinking about the most efficient way to get your clothes off between my front door and my bed. He was killing me.

When 5 p.m. finally arrived, I flew out of the office, keeping myself busy with a crossword puzzle and an upbeat playlist on the fifty-minute commute to the restaurant on 14th Street where I met up with Kat and Cam. For the first time all day, I was able to stop obsessing about the time as I lost myself in great conversation with my friends. We chatted about our birthdays, and Cam told us about the latest mismanagement nightmares at her office. She had some leads on other jobs in her industry— healthcare IT—and was desperate to find a new job.

Before we left, Cam and I visited the bathroom together. We were the only two in the room, so without bothering to cloister myself in a stall I yanked off my Spanx from under my dress, shoving them deep down in my considerable work purse, then spritzed myself with perfume.

Cam was laughing. "You're really going all out for this guy." She knew I didn't take off my Spanx, or my giant underpants for that matter, unless there was an important reason.

"I need to be able to get naked fast," I replied as I checked my teeth in the mirror and popped a mint in my mouth.

We took our time saying goodbye, each of us heading in different directions. But the second Cam and Kat were out of sight, I made a mad dash for the closest bus stop on 16th Street, just a few blocks away. I then texted Jed that I was on my way, and within thirty minutes I was kissing him beside his front door.

True to his word, he had me out of my clothes in no time and he spent the night tending, and re-tending, to my every need. Once or twice, I tried to cut in and offer him a turn, but he wouldn't hear of it.

We finally passed out around two or three in the morning. *So this is what it's like to be happy,* I mused with Jed's body wrapped around me. I had never been great at falling asleep with a guy touching me before. I usually preferred my space. But with Jed's body encasing mine, I fell into an easy sleep. When his alarm started chirping at 6:30 a.m., I thought it must be a mistake. It didn't take that long to make chocolate chip pancakes, the breakfast I had requested.

"Why are you getting up?" I mumbled as I saw him rise and pull on clothes.

"I just have a little something for you. Go back to bed. I'll wake you up in a bit." I heard the door to his apartment close behind him before I drifted back to sleep.

About thirty minutes later I felt Jed's hand on my arm. When my eyes focused, I realized he was sitting on the edge of the bed shirtless, holding a cup of Dunkin Donuts iced coffee, smiling at me. He had gotten up early and driven to the nearest Dunks to supply me with my preferred morning coffee. It was a simple gesture, but it struck a chord. In that moment, I felt a sense of joy I'd never experienced before.

Sipping my coffee, I followed Jed into the kitchen and watched him work. I loved watching him cook, and I loved how happy it made him to watch me enjoy his food.

Sitting on a stool at the counter in his kitchen—the only

space in his basement studio apartment where we could both eat—I enjoyed Jed's chocolatey pancakes and my delicious iced coffee. As I sipped, I thought that things really couldn't get any better.

"Are you almost done?" Jed interrupted my thoughts, though it was clear I hadn't yet finished the syrup-soaked pancakes on my plate. "I wanna go down on you again."

I dropped my fork mid-bite as he grabbed my hand and led me back to bed. It was only 8 a.m. We still had forty-five minutes to kill.

After the Dustin fiasco the previous summer, I had decided to hold off on sex until I had a clear read of the romantic situation. My experience with Chris had only reinforced that idea. *A ghoster doesn't deserve to get laid*, I reasoned to myself. But after my birthday, Jed and I couldn't keep our hands off each other. He respected my boundaries, arbitrary as they may have seemed to him. And we still managed to lose hours of our lives fooling around in bed.

I tried to continue online dating, to have other guys in the queue for when Jed inevitably disappeared, but it was a lost cause. Guys online, and anywhere else for that matter, fell short by comparison. Though he and I hadn't discussed exclusivity, I finally went online and disabled my OkCupid account.

The next few weeks were a blur of happiness unlike any I'd ever experienced. Jed and I saw each other three to four times a week, the hours between dates feeling unbearable despite the never-ending stream of always hilarious, occasionally sweet, texts.

Jed was incredible—witty, smart, attractive, thoughtful, extremely generous (in and out of bed), emotionally light years more mature than me. More than that, he made me feel incredible about myself and our relationship. In text and in person, he was completely up front about his feelings for me, reminding me often that he cared for me and missed me when I was away. Guys had told me similar empty platitudes in the past, only to disappear shortly after. But Jed stayed, and, unlike the others, I believed he was sincere. Rather than sit around with friends wasting time trying to decipher cryptic texts or vague references to future plans, as I had done before, I spent my time trying not to gush about this incredible new guy I was with. I had incorrectly assumed that all new couples started out on unsteady footing, that a poorly timed joke or misunderstood text was all it took to topple budding relationships. But with Jed, I found security. I trusted his words. I didn't have to decipher, just listen. And when we finally had the defining-the-relationship conversation, I was elated, but surprised by how unsurprised I was that he wanted to commit to me.

With each passing day, as it became more and more clear that Jed genuinely cared about me, it also became clear that none of the other guys I dated had. Not one. In retrospect, I couldn't believe I had wasted time on the Tucsons and ghosters of the world. I had only chased them because I didn't know there was something better. I hadn't known I could be better. But with Jed, I was.

Even when, shortly after we began dating exclusively, things began to get rocky in Jed's life, he still found ways to let me know that the slowdown in communication and date-frequency had nothing to do with me.

I had met Jed during the last month of his master's program studying Middle East policy at a local university.

As April drew to a close, the stress of finals, his impending oral comprehension exams, and his job hunt overwhelmed him. He understandably retreated into his schoolwork and job applications, but still texted me often to tell me how he wished we were together instead.

In early May, with his classes behind him and a passing grade on his oral comps, Jed found out he was the recipient of a competitive fellowship in the federal government. It was a prestigious program that accepted just a few hundred applicants each year after a grueling application and interview process. I was doubly excited. Not only would this fellowship allow him to compete for an exclusive group of jobs unavailable to the public, but I assumed it would boost his morale, which had been wavering.

And, for a moment, it did. He seemed energized about the job hunt, certain that his fellowship combined with his veteran status from his years in the Army would open doors for him. He even invited me to join him and his family for a tour of the White House when they visited for his graduation later that month. I had never been asked to meet a guy's family before. I rarely even met guys' friends. The invitation was unexpected and meaningful.

But the initial job applications he sent out seemed to get lost in the great USAjobs abyss—the website where resumes for federal jobs go to die. The lack of response to his applications affected him deeply. He tried harder, spending hours crafting cover letters, days applying to every job even remotely related to foreign policy. Still, he heard nothing. And, when his state Senator was unable to secure White House visitor passes for us, Jed made no further mention of me meeting his family when they came to DC.

In mid-May I began to feel uneasy for the first time since Jed and I had started dating. I hadn't once freaked out about our relationship, or questioned his feelings or his intentions, in the entire month and a half we'd been together. That was a record for me. But it felt like something was shifting.

I was leaving for a long weekend trip with Ainsley and Angela that Thursday and Jed had offered to drive me to the airport. My flight departed from BWI, located, as the name suggests, between Baltimore and Washington, DC, at 7 a.m. Since I was flying out in the morning, I suggested that I just spend Wednesday night at Jed's so we could leave straight from his place.

He picked me up around 9 p.m. the night before my trip and took me back to his apartment. Immediately upon walking in the door he mentioned that he was exhausted and would probably be turning in soon. We laid down on his couch together and watched a few episodes of *Veep*, his arm wrapped around my waist. By 10:30, he was in bed. I stripped down to my bra and underwear and crawled in next to him, hoping at least for a hot make-out session, but he just kissed my shoulder, rolled onto his side, and fell asleep.

He kissed me the next morning as we said goodbye at the airport, but it somehow felt empty. I spent the next several hours of my cross-country flight to Seattle aware that something was off between us, but unable to figure out what. Usually I get that uneasy feeling about a guy in that short time between when he's already ghosted me but before I've figured it out—those pathetic hours or days spent telling myself that there's still a chance I'll hear back from a guy, even though in my gut I know he's already deleted me from his phone.

I told Ainsley and Angela as much—that my whirlwind romance was likely ending soon. But when I returned to DC four days later, Jed and I just picked up where we left off. For the next few weeks, we both acted like things were normal. And sometimes they were. Some days he was full of passion and warmth; other days he was cold and distant. Still, conversation with him was always interesting and replete with witty banter. We had fun together. And though physically it felt like things were cooling off between us, I was still insanely attracted to him. I loved just being near him.

In early June, he thought he hit the jackpot when he was invited in for an interview at the US Department of State. But just two days after the interview, he received an auto-generated email informing him that he didn't get the job. He was crushed and starting to get a little desperate. He didn't have many other interviews lined up, and the GI Bill had stopped funding him after graduation. He was living on the wages he received from his part-time job working for one of his professors and the money he received from various family members as a graduation gift. That wasn't going to last long.

Two weeks later, when he was called into the exact same office at the State Department for a second interview, he was confused, but hopeful. He assumed the person they initially wanted to hire had turned them down or had been unable to accept the position. I received an excited text later that afternoon telling me they offered him the job, pending his security clearance. Not only did he have a job, but it was a job doing something he was excited about and qualified for. Neither of us could wait to celebrate.

In what I had assumed was a reaction to stress, Jed had been physically distant in the preceding weeks. But this job offer seemed to energize him. We met at a Mexican restaurant we both enjoyed in the nearby neighborhood of Columbia Heights to celebrate. We then headed to his place to hang out. I was about to take my usual place on his couch when he wrapped his arms around me and pulled me in for a lengthy kiss. I eagerly returned his kiss and took his hand, allowing myself to be guided to his bed. Generous as always, Jed worked his way up and down my body that night, and I felt all my recent relationship anxieties melt away. It was reassuring to know that he still wanted me, a notion I had been less sure of lately. And, for a little while at least, it felt like our relationship was back on track.

Unfortunately, our happiness was short-lived. A month after being offered the job and completing the necessary stacks of paperwork, Jed found out that the State Department hadn't even begun the security clearance process for him. And, upon further prodding, he was told it could be months before he was processed and cleared. That meant months without a paycheck and months without a daily routine or a purpose.

Though there's never a good time for a relationship to hit a serious rough patch, the timing was particularly hard for us. While it felt like I had known Jed forever, our relationship was still quite new. The truth was, I didn't know Jed well enough to know his response to stress, to know what he needed from me to help him cope. And every relationship I had had over the past few years had conditioned me to avoid discussions about feelings, to refrain from showing too much interest or trying to get too involved in a guy's life, lest he disappear. My few awkward attempts to talk to Jed about what was bothering him while also trying to keep things light and superficial only seemed to make him retreat further. As much as I wanted to pretend that I had hit a dating reset when I met Jed, it was clear the ghosters of my past were haunting me.

I could see Jed spinning and feel him pulling away, an all-too-familiar feeling for me. By July, our physical relationship was all but over—Jed was experiencing insomnia, so he was up most nights till he crashed in the early morning hours. And we were down to just two dates a week.

In August, he confided that he was in a depression, something he had briefly experienced once before while in the Army. He had tried medication at that time, to no avail, and he wasn't interested in giving meds another shot. I hoped he'd reconsider, but knew the decision was one he had to make for himself. Instead, I tried to be there for him in case he wanted to talk or discuss his options. He didn't. And, because of my emotional shortcomings, I didn't push the issue. The man who had been an open book, an amazing communicator, and completely in tune with his emotions when we first met was now silent on this, and most other issues relating to his health, which was starting to deteriorate. In addition to his insomnia, he was experiencing problems with his vision.

Despite all this, Jed still reached out. We texted daily, and Jed continued to make plans with me, to make me feel like a part of his life, even as it was unraveling. Unfortunately, our dates had become difficult to plan.

Though he had no source of income—his part-time job had ended with the arrival of the incoming class of students—Jed resented it when I paid for him. And, though DC is a city full of free activities, most of those free activities are museums or galleries that we had each been to a million times. We fell into a rut of cheap movies at the independent E Street Cinema downtown, watching TV at his place, and catching the occasional free comedy show at a local bar.

In late August, Jed went to the local VA Medical Center, now his only source of medical care, to get his eyes checked out. While there, the issue of his depression came up, and he begrudgingly mentioned that he'd be interested in talking to someone about it. But, living up to the VA's own terrible reputation, rather than set him up with counseling, they instead suggested he attend a goal-visualization workshop. Even then, they failed to follow up with him.

Dejected, he chose not to contact them further. And he resisted the idea of looking elsewhere for help. It was a tough situation, a friend of mine in the Army explained. Jed was depressed because the drawn-out security clearance process left him in a position of feeling useless, purposeless. But, at the same time, if he was found to be receiving treatment for a mental health issue, like depression, the clearance process could be prolonged even further as they investigated why he needed treatment. Or, his clearance request could be denied outright. He was being forced to suffer in silence or risk losing the job for which he was suffering. More than that, because of his depression he had no motivation to go out and look for other work, work that might have given him purpose and helped him heal. It was painful to watch as an outsider. I couldn't even imagine how excruciating it was to live.

For my part, I began to read everything I could about coping with a partner who has depression. Allie Brosh's *Hyperbole and a Half* blog entries about depression were the most eloquent, informative, and even humorous items I found. For about two weeks, I read them daily to remind myself that nothing I did or said could make Jed snap out of it. I understood that if I was going to see Jed through his depression, I couldn't take his isolation or lack of physical affection personally. I could be there for him, but I had to recognize that his depression was deeply personal. I couldn't make it about me. Inspired by other articles I read, I started leaving notes around his apartment and sending him cards with the intention of reminding him that he was still valued and cared for. But his reaction to those gestures, as with everything in his life, was muted. Though rationally I knew it was beyond my power to lift his spirits, I hated that I couldn't make him happy. Everything I said and did became shrouded in inadequacy. I felt like a terrible girlfriend for not knowing how to help him or even speak to him about what was going on.

During this time my friends, concerned for my well-being, counseled me to end my relationship with Jed. I knew his depression was affecting me, and my interactions with him often left me feeling lonely afterward. But I also knew that this amazing guy whom I adored, whom I had fallen in love with (despite never admitting this out loud for fear of losing him), was suffering. And though our relationship no longer felt romantic, he still managed to make me laugh, to make me smile in a way that few people could. I was determined to stick it out, to be his support if he decided to use me. "As long as I still feel like he wants me in his life, I'm going to be there for him," I told them.

We hadn't been together long, but Jed meant more to me than anyone I'd ever dated. He was proof that if I was willing to wait, to hold out and not sell myself short, I could find the person I wanted to spend every moment of every day with. He made me happy in a way I'd never experienced, and I wanted so badly to be there to make him that happy too.

I had mistakenly thought we'd already reached our lowest point, that if we just held on a little longer, things would inevitably get better. But in mid-September, the bottom dropped out. I was at work when I received a text from Jed letting me know that his interim security clearance, the clearance the government could have granted him so he could start working while they finished investigating him fully, had been denied for reasons unknown. I burst into tears at my desk, realizing for the first time that Jed was going to be unemployed and therefore depressed for the foreseeable future. The interim clearance had been the only remaining thread of hope. Through tears, I texted my friend Caroline: *Jed didn't get the interim clearance. Our relationship won't survive this.*

Immediately, the frequency of texts and emails dropped to almost nothing. For the first time since his depression set in, I couldn't tell if Jed cared about me or even wanted me in his life. As he withdrew further, I went into survival mode and began to emotionally prepare myself for the impending breakup. But it didn't come. After an intervention, and more than a bit of whiskey, with several friends, I came to terms with the fact that I would have to ask Jed point blank if he still cared about me. I couldn't put myself through the constant emotional drain for someone who had become indifferent to me. I also didn't want him to feel trapped, to stay with me simply because it was easier than dealing with a breakup on top of everything else he was experiencing.

Jed and I met outside the E Street Cinema, a small theater downtown that showed a mix of indie, foreign, and popular films, on a rainy evening in late September. We had planned to see a documentary about the Vietnam War, but I had suggested we arrive early so we could take a pre-movie walk. The sidewalks were mostly deserted due to the weather, and two blocks into our walk, I found the courage to ask him the question I had been dreading: "Do you still want to be in this relationship?"

"I guess that's something we should talk about, huh?" His response said it all. I felt like the blood had drained from my body.

In preparing for the talk, I anticipated that the conversation could go one of two ways: 1) Jed would acknowledge that things were rough, but say that he still very much wanted to be with me, even if he couldn't show it at the moment, or 2) Jed would tell me that it was over. Since I'm terrible at dealing with and communicating emotions and was afraid I might react poorly to the latter scenario, I had rehearsed parts of it earlier that afternoon, preparing for what Jed might say. Oddly, instead of being overwhelmed by emotion, I just felt numb. As I stared blankly at the old brick facade of an office building on the next block, I found myself reciting my rehearsed lines from rote. Blood must have been rushing through my head at that point; Jed's voice sounded muffled though he was standing beside me. The conversation felt far away, like I was watching from a distance rather than participating. I can't remember the full conversation. I'm not even sure I heard it all. But the pieces I remember are of him reassuring me he still enjoyed my company, but that being in a relationship to which he didn't feel like he was contributing made him feel worthless. I have no idea if that's truly what he said; maybe that's just how I rewrote it in my mind. After all, it's easier to accept than "I just don't care about you anymore."

We decided to skip the movie, and he walked me back to the Metro station, making banal conversation the whole way. I tuned out as he prattled on about *The Skeleton Twins*, a movie that was about to be released and starred Kristen Wiig in an unusual dramatic role. I knew Jed was depressed, but in that moment I desperately and irrationally needed him to feel something. Anything. Instead, he looked at me the way he always did with those beautiful hazel eyes, no acknowledgement that anything had changed between us. If anything, he seemed relieved. And as we stood atop the Metro Center station escalator, he apologized for the breakup the way he might apologize for over-salting one of the delicious meals he used to make for me. In the same monotone, he asked if we could still be friends. Still numb, I told him I needed to think about that.

As I wrapped my arms around him one last time, every emotion I had bottled up over the previous several months was released. I turned my back on him and was halfway down the escalator before the tears began. I sobbed all the way home, not caring what the strangers on the train, on the sidewalks, or in my building thought.

By the time I collapsed on my bed that night, I knew that I would accept Jed's proposal to remain friends. Like the people on *The Price is Right* who get called from the audience but never make it on stage and are sent home with a Cuisinart or a year's supply of ham, it was something, but it wasn't what I was playing for. Jed's friendship would be my consolation prize. But the Jed I knew, the one I had loved, was long gone.

On my worst days following my breakup with Jed, I felt hopeless. It had taken the better part of a decade, but I had *finally* met an incredible man, convinced him to fall for me no less, and yet I still somehow found myself alone and miserable. I felt that maybe real, sustainable happiness wasn't in the cards for me. I didn't have the emotional or mental fortitude to wait another decade or longer for my next Jed. And even if I was lucky enough to find one, I'd be in my forties by then. It would be unlikely I'd ever have a family of my own. I wanted children, but I also knew I didn't want them badly enough to do it on my own. I darkly wondered which of my relatives and friends would be stuck caring for me in my old age.

In my brief moments of non-misery, as I went through the motions, waiting for that "time heals all wounds" crap to take effect, I managed to feel gratitude—that I had been cared for by an incredible man, that I had briefly experienced genuine happiness, that love was still a possibility for me, even if only temporarily. If nothing else, thanks to Jed, I finally knew what I was looking for and that it was achievable. I wasn't going to settle for anything less.

MY NEW NORMAL

Growing up, I had heard that the best way to get a guy's attention was to act uninterested, play hard-to-get. I had shrugged that off as childish advice. I preferred the straightforward tactic of telling a guy I was interested in him and waiting for his inevitable disappearance. But in the months following my breakup with Jed, I found out just how effective acting aloof was as a dating strategy.

Out of the blue, men began to surface around me like sharks hunting a wounded seal. Men I worked with, men I volunteered with, men I socialized with, random men singing karaoke at bars, men who had no idea I had been dating someone or that I was newly single, lined up to ask me out. It's like they could sense I was vulnerable and possibly willing to make poor decisions.

Though I wasn't interested in any of them, I gave many of them a chance, a date or two in the hope that I might feel something again. The reality was that I just wasn't ready. My stock was on the rise, but my interest had abated. But, the more I resisted, the harder I was pursued. Several men with whom I had declined second or third dates actively campaigned for another chance. I was honest with all of them, explaining that I was getting over a breakup and genuinely wasn't interested. To that, a few told me they'd be willing to wait it out, to hang out as friends—just friends, they swore—till I was emotionally ready to date again. They confidently boasted that I'd come around if I just spent more time with them. I had never had guys work so hard for a date. And I had never been less interested. Had I actually been willing and enticed, I suspect most of them would have ended up in Tucson.

In those months following the breakup, I also decided to take the time I used to waste dating ghosters, liars, and guys with whom I was just clearly incompatible, and channel it into self-improvement activities. Namely, fitness. Despite working out regularly since my move to Atlanta in 2010, maintaining a healthy weight was still a daily struggle. I had finally moved down the BMI chart from "obese" to "overweight" (celebratory Ben & Jerry's, anyone?), but I wanted very much to be in the "normal" weight category. As I amped up my workouts, I found that not only was I slowly losing weight and gaining strength, but the discomfort I felt when pushing myself at the gym temporarily relieved my sadness in those moments. Instead of sitting around wishing that I could text Jed about whatever mundane event had happened during my day, I could focus on the physical pain of running. If I felt spontaneous tears coming on because a TV show or a joke reminded me of happier times spent with Jed, I'd grab my weights and curse my way through a particularly painful upper body workout. Realizing that I couldn't simultane-ously miss Jed and run five grueling miles, I started spending more time at the gym. The longer I worked out, the fewer hours were left in the day for self-pity. And, as a bonus, the more I pushed myself, the more exhausted I became. Instead of restless nights spent fantasizing about Jed—his eyes, his kiss, his arms wrapped around me—I simply climbed into bed and passed out, wiped. Don't get me wrong, there were still plenty of hours each day devoted to missing him. But I had found a way to ensure the thoughts weren't all-consuming.

After just a few short months of a slightly obsessive exercise regimen, plus diet and dating moderation, I had dropped twenty pounds, gained tiny muscles that you could actually see (when I flexed really hard and pulled the excess skin out of the way), and was in the best shape of my life. I had finally achieved "normal." For the first time in my adult life, I was physically, though by no means emotionally, healthy.

Loneliness is still a pervasive feeling in my life, but most days it's just a soft hum in the background rather than the deafening roar I experienced for so long. It took a while, but I've learned I can't force a relationship into existence. I need to live my life and maybe, just maybe, I'll meet someone amazing.

Jed, who finally received his security clearance a full twelve months after applying for it, is my gold standard. I still haven't found anyone quite like him, but I do continue to date, just much more selectively. I don't know when I'll find love again—it could be a month from now, a year, a decade. And finding a love that lasts no longer feels like an inevitability. But thanks to Jed, I know that if I do find it, it will have been worth the wait. In the meantime, I'm sure there's more ghosting in my future. It's unavoidable. But for every ghost, there's a story. And sometimes a girl just needs a good story.

About Atmosphere Press

Atmosphere Press is an independent, full-service publisher for excellent books in all genres and for all audiences. Learn more about what we do at atmospherepress.com.

We encourage you to check out some of Atmosphere's latest releases, which are available at Amazon.com and via order from your local bookstore:

In Pursuit of Calm, by Daniel Fuselier, PsyD

UFOs of the Kickapoo, by John Sime

Livin' on the Edge: A Guide to Your Abundance Seeds, by Tinker McAdams

Purveyors of Light and Shadow: Two Artists Search For Meaning, by Kate Klein Calder

There Are Some Secrets, by Sara Sass

Running Away From the Circus: Confessions of a Carnie Kid (Who Tried to become a Priest), by Nove Meyers

Mama: True Stories of Maternal Health in Malawi, by Caitlin Arlene

Out and Back: Essays on a Family in Motion, by Elizabeth Templeman

About the Author

Jana Eisenstein is a writer. Ok, so prior to *Ghosted: Dating & Other Paramoural Experiences* no one technically paid for her writing, but it's what she loves to do. Growing up, she idolized Dave Barry and, as an adult, she thirsts for anything Tina Fey creates. When she's not writing or working her day job, she spends her time traveling (unless there's a pandemic), dancing (poorly), trying to convince herself that she enjoys running (unsuccessfully), and dating (when she needs a good laugh, or a good cry).